COOLING TOWERS
principles and practice

COOLING TOWERS
principles
and practice

a practical guide to Cooling Tower
selection and operation

W. STANFORD
C.Eng., M.I.Mech.E., M.I.H.V.E., A.M.A.S.H.R.E.

G. B. HILL
C.Eng., B.Sc., A.M.Inst.F.

First Edition 1967

Second Edition 1970
Reprinted 1972

© 1967, 70, 72 Carter Industrial Products Ltd.

SBN 902738 00 3

Published by
Carter Industrial Products Limited, Redhill Road, Hay Mills, Birmingham B25 8EY

Printed in England

foreword

This new edition comes at a time when the importance of re-using water is becoming more and more widely appreciated by industrialists and engineers.

Water is a commodity which is not in such plentiful supply that it may be thrown away haphazardly. Increasing costs of abstraction and treatment make it, in many cases, a commodity to be preserved and used with care.

On the other hand, users of water for cooling have a responsibility to the community; the careless rejection of unwanted heat to rivers and waterways can be a serious source of harm, sometimes described as thermal pollution.

Against this dual background, the publication of the second edition of this useful book for users of cooling towers is particularly appropriate. It should be of great assistance to those concerned with the specification and design or operation and maintenance of cooling towers whether for process plant, refrigeration, air conditioning or other purposes.

G. M. BERESFORD HARTWELL,
C.Eng., M.I.Mech.E., M.Inst.M.C., M.I.Nuc.E.,
Consulting Engineer,
Chairman of Council — Cooling Water Association.

contents

ILLUSTRATIONS CONTAINED IN TEXT

PLATES

LIST OF TABLES

CONVERSION TABLES

introduction
to the first edition

In many industrial processes unwanted heat is produced, the removal of which is vital to the successful operation of the equipment. For example, in internal combustion engines water is passed to the cylinder blocks to prevent excessive temperature rise of the cylinder walls; in machine tools oil is used to cool cutting tools; and air compressors are usually water cooled. Sometimes the removal of heat is an end result of an engineering process. In refrigeration circuits, for instance, heat is removed in the condenser.

Where water is used for cooling it must either be run to waste after use, or cooled before being recirculated. The cooling of the water may be carried out in various ways. Cooling ponds are sometimes used but, for various reasons, are rarely satisfactory. Air cooled water coolers can cool water down to only relatively high temperatures. Therefore, the commonest, and most efficient, device used for cooling water is the Evaporative Cooling Tower.

The Cooling Tower has come a very long way since its early days when manufacturers had little understanding of the mechanisms of heat transfer taking place in their products. In many instances, the result was towers grossly over-sized or quite inadequate for the specified duty.

But in recent years, to meet the ever increasing demand for the cooling of many and varied process engineering applications, design advances have been both dramatic and continuous. New materials have been developed to produce packs with a high resistance to deterioration and which can easily be cleaned; recessed fan housings are often used to produce a low silhouette to meet architectural requirements; noise level control has been improved; modular construction has simplified on site assembly; lightweight glass-fibre towers have been developed to facilitate roof-top installation.

Today, the emphasis is on the provision of dependable, compact, easily installed cooling towers, which require the minimum of maintenance. New materials and new manufacturing techniques have combined to produce these specifications. Further research into production methods and assembling routines is achieving significant reductions in production, transport and installation costs.

I

The Cooling Tower as an aid to water conservation

It is in the national interest for industry to practice water conservation, but there are also sound financial reasons for individual companies to assess the overall cost of water wastage, which, in many instances, is needlessly allowed to reach a figure of many thousands of pounds per annum.

Sometimes, mains water may be used because the requirements appear too small to merit the installation of a recirculatory cooling water system, or there may be space limitations that seem to preclude the use of a cooling tower. Often, the reason is the mistaken belief that it is cheaper to waste water than to purchase and install a cooling tower, then subsequently pay for its operation.

It is, however, a proven fact that, for virtually every application, a cooling tower can be installed and operated for a good deal less than the total annual bill that would otherwise have to be paid for mains water. In fact, the more mains water that is at present being used, the greater the saving that could be made by the employment of a cooling tower.

This book deals with the theory and practice of the Cooling Tower. Its co-authors have attempted to ensure that it will play a useful part in facilitating an understanding of the selection and operation of this important piece of equipment. It is hoped that the method of presentation will enable the reader to assimilate quickly the main principles, so that he will fully realise the possibilities for the use of the Cooling Tower in reducing production costs.

introduction
to the second edition

The Second Edition of this book is substantially as before with the following exceptions:—

1. The chapter on noise theory has been dropped but the chapter on noise from cooling towers has been completely rewritten and expanded.

2. The chapter on water treatment has been completely rewritten and expanded.

3. A chapter on the determination of cooling duties has been added to the theory section.

Careful consideration was given to changing to S.I. units but it was finally decided that this would be premature.

The authors acknowledge, on the opposite page, the assistance given by others in the preparation of this book but, of course, all errors and omissions remain the responsibility of the authors.

acknowledgments

The Authors are grateful for the expert assistance provided by the Water Treatment Division of Forestal Industries (UK) Limited in the preparation of the completely new chapter on water treatment. Acknowledgments of copyrights are made covering extracts from a publication in course of preparation covering multi-phase water treatment and entitled "The Industrial Use of Water".

A number of points on cooling tower biology in various parts of the book have been corrected or clarified with the expert advice of the Forest Products Research Laboratory, Princes Risborough, for which assistance the authors are extremely grateful.

The Authors are indebted to F. Reynolds, F.S.H., M.A.P.H.I., M.Inst.F., Chief Air Pollution and Noise Abatement Officer of the City of Birmingham for his assistance in the preparation of the new chapter on noise from cooling towers.

The Authors wish to express their gratitude to T. G. Martin, T.D., M.I.Mech.E., F.I.E.E., for his many excellent suggestions and the provision of valuable additional material.

They also acknowledge the invaluable assistance of J. R. Taylor of Carter Industrial Products Limited, Cooling Tower Division, in collecting and preparing material for this book.

A number of major cooling tower manufacturers have kindly permitted us to include photographs of their cooling towers and these are duly acknowledged under each photograph.

The Authors also wish to thank the undermentioned for permission to reproduce the following: British Compressed Air Society — Table 7. (from their "Reference Book"); — Foster Wheeler Ltd. — Fig. 15 (from "Cooling Towers" by J. Jackson, B.Sc.); Elsevier Publishing Co. Ltd. — Fig. 5 (from "The Industrial Cooling Tower," by McKelvey & Brooke) with acknowledgments to The Davenport Engineering Co., Bradford; to Koninklijke Nederlandse Akadamic van Wetenschappen, Amsterdam and to The Marley Co., Kansas City and the "Petroleum Engineer"; Kinnis & Brown Limited — "Scale Formation in Pipes"; Wellman Incandescent Ltd. — Fig. 36; Institute of Heating & Ventilating Engineers — Fig. 44 (from "I.H.V.E. Guide 1965"; Institute of Mechanical Engineers — Fig. 49 (from "Proceedings 153 (1950)" by Carey & Williamson).

SECTION 1 — practice

chapter 1

COOLING TOWER FUNDAMENTALS

Main Components
Operating Terms
Fundamental Principles

1. Cooling Tower Fundamentals

The Cooling Tower has been defined elsewhere as "an enclosed device for the evaporative cooling of water by contact with air". This might seem to be an over simplification, but in fact, Cooling Towers are, physically, relatively simple devices, and the enclosure referred to may be little more than a four-sided wooden structure.

However, although the basic structure of a Cooling Tower can be easily described and understood, the heat transfer processes which take place within a tower are extremely complex.

Examples of steel panelled, multi-cell cooling towers showing relative simplicity of basic structure.

To begin with, certain definitions and an explanation of some of the terms which will be encountered are necessary. A typical tower arrangement, with the main components indicated is shown in Fig. 1. It should be noted that not all towers are of this type. The various types of tower will be explained in Chapter 2.

MAIN COMPONENTS

Casing or Shell. This is the structure which encloses the heat transfer process. In practice, it also usually provides a support for the other main items.

Air Inlet and Outlet. The positions at which air enters and leaves the tower.

Fan. In Mechanical (as opposed to Natural) Draught Towers, a fan is provided to move the required amount of air through the water to be cooled.

Drift Eliminators. These are positioned at, or near, the air outlet and prevent droplets of water from being carried from the tower by the airstream.

Water Inlet. This is the point at which water enters the tower.

Water Distribution System. For maximum effect, the water entering the tower must be spread evenly over the top of the packing. It is to achieve this that the distribution system is used. There are a variety of distribution systems available: sprays where nozzles are used to atomise the water; or trough and weir where the water spreads by gravity. Some common examples of distribution system types are shown in Figs. 2a-2d.

Packing. In order to provide a large water surface area to assist heat transfer, a number of baffles are placed within the casing of the tower. These baffles form the packing which is so arranged that the air and water, which must pass through it, come into direct contact in the process. There are a great many different types of packing in use and these will be described later in the book.

Tank or Sump. This is provided at the base of the tower and is often integral with the casing. Its function is to collect the cooled water before it is returned to the process which it is cooling.

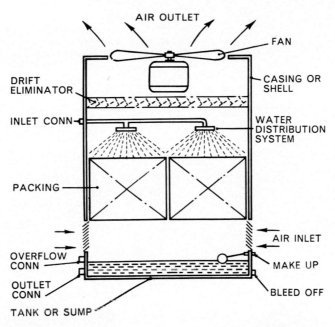

Fig. 1. Schematic arrangement of a typical mechanical draught cooling tower.

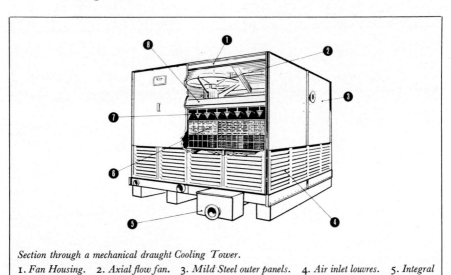

Section through a mechanical draught Cooling Tower.
1. Fan Housing.   2. Axial flow fan.   3. Mild Steel outer panels.   4. Air inlet louvres.   5. Integral sump.   6. Packing.   7. Water distributors.   8. Spray eliminators.

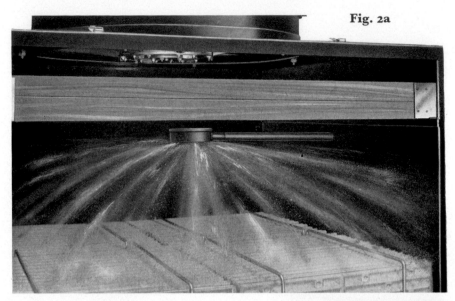

Fig. 2a

Fig. 2c

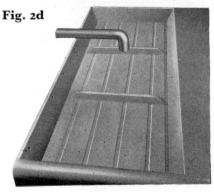

Fig. 2d

Fig. 2b

Types of water distribution system.

Fig. 2a. Spray type.
Fig. 2b. Trough.
Fig. 2c. Perforated pipe.
Fig. 2d. Perforated pan.

OPERATING TERMS

Cooling Range. This is the difference between the water temperatures entering and leaving the tower.

Approach. The difference between the temperature of the water leaving the tower, and the wet bulb temperature of the air entering. It is impossible to cool water below the wet bulb temperature of the air with which it is in contact. In fact, the smaller this difference, the more arduous the cooling duty, and in practice, the cooling tower supplier will often design for the greatest approach for which the relevant re-cooled temperature is acceptable to the client. A "close approach" is 5°F, though a very few towers have been designed to operate at less. A more common approach for towers to be located in mid-England is 7-15°F.

Cooling Load. This is the rate at which heat is removed from the water. In this country it is usually expressed in Btu per hr. and it is given by the product of the amount of water in circulation in lb. per hr. and the cooling range in °F.

Purge. As water circulates, evaporates and is replaced, the impurities contained in the make-up water tend to concentrate in the system. Therefore, a deliberate intermittent, or continuous, discharge is bled to drain to prevent the precipitation of solids, and thus formation of scale. In determining the purge rate, the cooling tower designer (or water treatment specialist) will require to know the tower duty and water analysis.

Make-up. Since the tower cools by evaporating some of the circulating water, it follows that the quantity circulating in the cooling system would gradually diminish unless steps were taken to replenish it. Even when drift eliminators are used, some water is carried away in the outlet air in the form of droplets, and this also must be replaced. In addition, enough water must be deliberately bled to drain to ensure that chemical solids do not rise to unacceptable levels.

The total water lost from these three causes, viz., evaporation, drift and purge, is the quantity required to be fed into the system as fresh make-up. The amount of make-up required will depend on a number of factors, including water temperature level, but is usually between 3% and 5% in a well designed tower.

FUNDAMENTAL PRINCIPLES

Consider a droplet of water inside the tower. As shown in Fig. 3, this droplet will be surrounded by a thin film of air. As air flows past the droplet, heat is transferred in three ways:—

(a) By radiation from the surface of the droplet; this is a very small proportion of the total amount of heat flow and it is usually neglected.

(b) By conduction and convection between water and air; the amount of heat transferred will depend on the temperatures of air and water. It is a significant proportion of the whole, and may be as much as one-quarter to one-third.

(c) By evaporation; this accounts for the majority of heat transfer and is the reason why the whole process is termed "Evaporative Cooling".

In view of the importance of evaporation in a cooling tower, it is necessary to subject it to closer scrutiny.

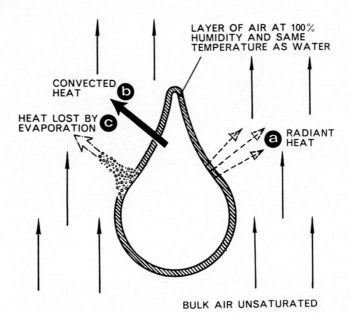

Fig. 3. Diagram showing the various ways in which a water droplet loses heat.

The evaporation that occurs when air and water are in contact, is caused by the difference in pressures of water vapour at the surface of the water and in the air. These vapour pressures are functions of the water temperature and the degree of saturation of the air, respectively.

In a cooling tower, the water and air streams are generally opposed so that cooled water leaving the bottom of the pack is in contact with the entering air. Similarly, hot water entering the pack will be in contact with warm air leaving the pack.

Evaporation will take place throughout the pack. It should be noted, that at the top of the pack, the fact that the air is nearly saturated, is compensated for by the high water temperature and consequently high vapour pressure.

The amount of evaporation which takes place depends on a number of factors, including the total surface area the water presents to the air (which is why the pack design is so important) and the amount of air flowing. The greater the airflow, the more cooling is achieved.

This is because as the air rate increases, the effect of the water on it will become less, and the partial pressure differences throughout the pack will be increased.

The wet bulb temperature of the entering air has a very important effect. A lower wet bulb temperature produces a lower water-off temperature.

The factors which influence the performance of a cooling tower may be summarised as follows:

(i)   The cooling range.

(ii)   The approach.

(iii)   The ambient wet bulb temperature.

(iv)   The flow rate of the water to be cooled (or circulation rate).

(v)   The rate at which air is passed over the water.

(vi)   The temperature level.

(vii) The performance coefficient of the packing to be used.

(viii) The volume of packing (i.e. height multiplied by horizontal cross-sectional area).

(ix)   The type of water distribution system.

Item (vi) is important because of the exponential nature of the saturation line of the psychrometric chart as (for a given range and approach) much greater cooling can be achieved at higher temperature levels.

Items (vii) and (viii) are self-evident, as, by definition, the performance of the pack is directly related to each.

In modern cooling towers, the water distribution system, Item (ix), is responsible for only a very small part of the total cooling range.

However, with the atmospheric type tower and other cases where no packing is used in conjunction with spray type distribution, it is obviously of considerable importance.

chapter 2

TYPES OF COOLING TOWER

Natural Draught

Mechanical Draught

Contra-Flow

Cross-Flow

Forced and Induced Draught

2. Types of Cooling Tower

There are a great many different types of cooling tower used in industry, but they can be divided into two main categories, depending upon the method by which air is moved through the tower.

1. Natural Draught Towers

As the name implies, these rely upon natural forces to move air through the pack. They can be subdivided into two types: (*a*) atmospheric; (*b*) chimney.

Those of type (*a*) are sometimes known as "frames" rather than towers and few of these are in demand today. Those of type (*b*) are generally either of the timber penthouse type or of the concrete hyperbolic pattern; the latter are very much taller and are commonly used in European Power Stations and Steelworks. Fig. 4.

Atmospheric "frames" are the simplest type of tower, consisting of little more than a shell containing a spray system. This shell is tall and narrow, the long sides having louvres which are exposed to prevailing winds, so that air enters and mixes with the water spray.

In the direction of air flow, the shell is relatively narrow so that the path the air takes is short and resistance low, ensuring maximum air flow for a given wind velocity.

Due to the large area presented to the prevailing wind by these towers careful design is necessary to prevent them collapsing in high winds.

An additional disadvantage, is that the tower is dependent not only on air temperatures, but on wind velocity and direction for its thermal performance. Consequently, it is impossible to control water temperatures with any degree of accuracy.

Better control is obtained with the chimney type of tower in which air movement is much less dependent on wind velocity or direction.

This is a "Packed" tower, that is, one where a grid arrangement in the body of the tower presents a large surface area of contact between air and water for better cooling.

Air is induced vertically through the tower by convection, the air inside the tower being warmer (and therefore less dense) than the surrounding atmosphere. These towers are cheap to run compared with mechanical

Fig. 4. Group of concrete hyperbolic natural draught cooling towers.

Fig. 5. Timber construction natural draught cooling tower.

draught towers even allowing for the increased pumping head, but they occupy a large area and are very high compared with more conventional types.

Their capacity for handling very large water flow rates makes them particularly suitable for power station and similar applications where their size is not a disadvantage, and where cooling ranges are modest and approach temperatures are wide.

The hyperbolic tower is usually constructed in concrete, although timber and asbestos-cement have been used. When timber is used the design is more often as shown in Fig. 5.

Few towers of this type are built today because of the many disadvantages. Some of these are:—

(1) The practical limit in height of a timber tower is about 70 feet. Above this height, joints in the very important columns or masts seriously threaten strength in a high wind.

(2) There is a fire risk, especially in towers which are dry from non-use at certain times of year, e.g., during periods of plant overhaul.

(3) For large water flows, several towers become more practicable than a single very large tower and this sometimes creates siting problems.

2. Mechanical Draught Towers

Usually, in industry, the need is for a tower occupying minimum ground or roof space and to cool water to lower re-cooled temperatures than is easily done by natural draught towers. Mechanical draught towers are, therefore, employed in nearly all modern industrial process cooling. They have the added advantages of not possessing dominating heights and also not requiring high pumping heads. Additionally, they offer some facility in water temperature control.

This type of tower incorporates a fan which provides a steady flow of air through the packing, making the dependence upon atmospheric conditions even less; whereas the atmospheric tower is completely dependent upon weather conditions, and water temperatures vary with wind velocity and direction. This dependence is reduced in the chimney type but the amount of air induced decreases with increases in ambient dry bulb temperatures.

In the mechanical draught tower virtually the only atmospheric factor affecting performance is wet bulb temperature.

The provision of fans permits a relatively high rate of air flow and consequently a smaller tower for a given duty. Also control of water temperature by fan regulation is possible.

Smaller and more compact towers can be used, often situated on the roof of a building, or in a plant room. In fact, they can be positioned without regard to wind direction, degree of exposure or other factors which need consideration in the case of a natural draught tower.

Water temperature can be controlled reasonably accurately by regulating the amount of air passing through the tower, by fan speed using control, either by two-speed motors or by use of adjustable impeller vanes and a single-speed motor. Both methods are inexpensive though the cost of the former rises for a wide speed range. (For a fair comparison, the cost of duplicate cabling to motor stator windings and the expense of more complex starters or controllers for motor circuits must be taken into account.) More frequently, towers are provided with multiple fans and these may be switched on and off in sequence by a thermostat, as more or less cooling is required. Fig. 6.

Higher air velocities than can be achieved by natural convection and wind forces can be used in a mechanical draught tower. By this means, the cooling effect can be increased. At the same time, packing of a higher density (with a much larger surface area) can be used with similar results. Water loss can be kept to the minimum by correctly designed and efficient spray eliminators, as the resulting resistance to air flow can be overcome by the fan. The water that does get away is largely vapour which is unavoidable and *not* droplets which is undesirable.

One of the major advantages of the mechanical draught tower, is that it can cool to lower water temperatures than a natural draught tower. Additionally, the mechanical draught tower will cool more easily through much larger temperature ranges.

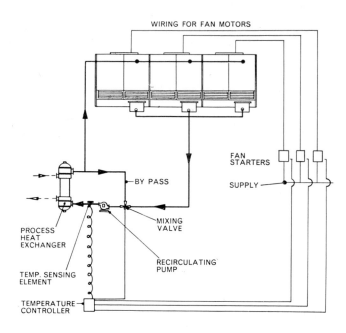

Fig. 6. Typical method of controlling temperature of water leaving a multi-cell cooling tower.

The fans need to be driven (nearly always electric motors are used), therefore maintenance and operating costs are higher than for a natural draught tower. However, operating costs are offset to some extent by the reduced pump horsepower due to the lower height, and by the saving, generally substantial, in capital cost compared with a natural draught tower.

Mechanical draught towers can be divided into a number of different types, but the two main types are classified according to the relationship between the directions of movement of the air and water.

(a) Contra-Flow Towers

Air and water flow in opposite directions in this type, the water falling by gravity over the packing and the air passing vertically upwards.

In this arrangement, cooled water leaving the pack meets air at its coldest and driest condition. As the air passes through the pack it collects heat and moisture, and at the top of the pack it is in contact with hot water entering the tower. This arrangement has been found to give best results for a given set of conditions.

These towers may be subdivided into two groups depending upon whether the fan handles inlet or outlet air. These are known as Forced Draught and Induced Draught towers respectively, and are shown diagrammatically in Figs. 7a and 7b.

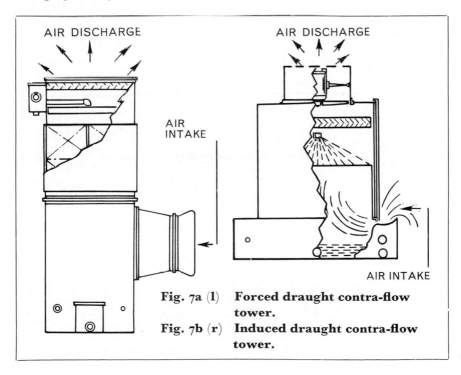

Fig. 7a (l) Forced draught contra-flow tower.

Fig. 7b (r) Induced draught contra-flow tower.

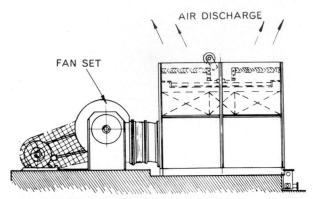

Fig. 8. Forced draught contra-flow tower with centrifugal fan.

The forced draught tower was the first mechanical draught tower in general use, although it is less frequently used today. As shown, the fan is mounted below the pack, delivering ambient air to the tower. It was this fact which led to its popularity, as in those early days electric motors were extremely unreliable in the humid air found at the tower outlet. The low cost arrangement of an axial flow impeller mounted on a motor shaft was therefore suitable for forced draft towers.

An alternative to the axial flow fan, is the centrifugal fan, which does not lend itself to induced draught applications, but which can be employed on

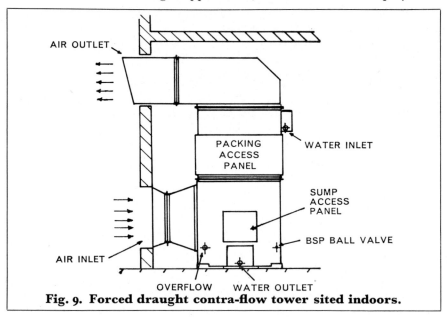

Fig. 9. Forced draught contra-flow tower sited indoors.

forced draught towers where the much higher cost is justified by the lower noise characteristic (see Fig. 8). Noise attenuators for axial flow fans can sometimes be provided by specialists but disadvantages of their use are higher cost and increased motor rating from the higher airflow resistance.

One disadvantage of the centrifugal fan is the large floor area which it occupies; although this can be reduced to some extent by using double-width double-inlet types with their correspondingly smaller diameters.

A feature of forced draught towers (with both types of fan) is that the configuration lends itself to applications where it is desirable to house the tower indoors and where there is an outside wall (see Fig. 9).

An additional feature of greater value, perhaps, is that forced draught towers are nearly always of less height than induced draught towers and this fact commends itself where towers must be concealed, though this asset must be weighed against the commonly met risk of recirculation of saturated air.

Forced draught towers, having fan masses at the bottom, suffer much less from vibration and structural weaknesses developing therefrom, than do induced draught towers.

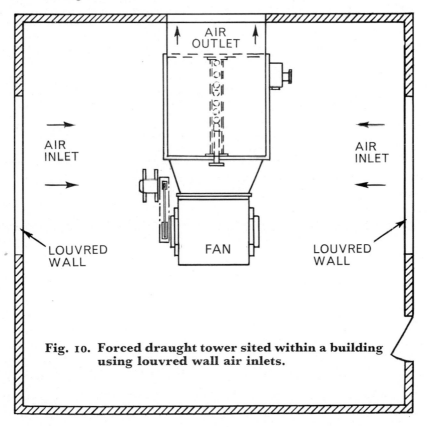

Fig. 10. Forced draught tower sited within a building using louvred wall air inlets.

With the double-width centrifugal fan, ducting from the fan inlets to atmopshere is a complication. Usually the towers are sited outside, or in a plant room with air intake louvres fitted in the outside wall (see Fig. 10).

There are some disadvantages with forced draught towers, the main being:—

(1) Hot saturated air, discharged at a low velocity at the top of the tower, may easily be entrained in the high velocity airstream of the fan inlet, reducing the effectiveness of the tower. Recirculation is still more likely where vapour deflection from an adjoining building or where downward gusts of wind are features of the site.

(2) Larger plan areas are required than with induced draught, though with induced draught the air intake louvres must be unobstructed.

(3) As the air inlet is on one side, the height of the tower increases with fan diameter although the packing height is constant. To keep within economic and practical limits it is necessary to limit the size of the tower.

(4) Conditions at the fan inlet can result in ice formation; with centrifugal fans this is not a serious problem but it can cause extensive damage in the case of the axial flow fan. The danger is that ice will bridge between the blade tips and the casing when the fan is stationary, with a possible motor burn-out when an attempt is made to re-start. An upward tilted fan is usual to minimise this hazard though it causes an increase in the likelihood of recirculation at times of wind change.

The majority of contra-flow towers now being installed are of the induced draught type, and because of the cost of using centrifugal fans they are usually fitted with axial flow fans. In addition, centrifugal fans are not available in such large diamters as axial flow fans. Both types are illustrated, Fig. 11a is a conventional tower with axial fan, Fig. 11b shows an induced draught, contra-flow tower with a centrifugal fan (note filters on air inlets).

As cooling tower packing designs progress the air pressure drops diminish. There are rare tower designs in which packing pressure drop is rather high for axial flow fans.

As shown in these illustrations, the fan is situated at the top of the tower, and the air intake louvres are fitted in the four sides below the packing. This configuration leads to an evenly distributed air flow through the packing with a better heat exchange between air and water.

In plan, the fan is confined within the outline of the tower sides. Even allowing an air passage to the louvres, the floor area is less than would be necessary for a forced draught tower. Similarly, the louvre height is comparatively small but usually the induced draught tower presents a higher silhouette on account of the space necessary between the water distribution system and the fan for safe access for maintenance. It will be appreciated that obstructions from adjacent plant or structures may preclude air inlets on one, two or three sides in which case the tower height is increased correspondingly as the reduced number of air inlets are heightened to maintain an acceptable air entry velocity.

Fig. 11a. Carter Universal induced draught contra-flow tower, showing internals.

In most cases, the axial flow impeller is mounted on the shaft of the driving motor but on very large towers where fan diameters of 12 ft/15 ft and speeds of only 200/300 rpm are used, this is not possible, and the method usually adopted is to drive the fan through a gear box.

In contrast to the forced draught tower there is a low velocity at the intake louvres and a high velocity at the fan outlet. Consequently, there is little danger of moist air being recirculated.

It should be noted that the large, evenly spaced air inlets assist natural draught when the fans cut out under thermostatic control or are stopped due to a mechanical or electrical failure. In such events most induced draught towers will operate with 25-30% of the design cooling duty but at a wider approach temperature.

(b) Cross-Flow Towers

In the cross-flow tower, water falls vertically, by gravity, over the packing and air flows horizontally. There are forced and induced draught types which are illustrated.

Fig. 11b. Induced draught contra-flow tower with centrifugal fan and air inlet filters.

Fig. 12a shows the forced draught type which is rarely used, other than for very small duties. The induced draught (Fig. 12b) is more often encountered, usually in the form shown in Fig. 13, where twin packs either side of the fan give a very compact arrangement.

Because the tower height is little more than that of the packing a lower silhouette is possible than with a contra-flow tower (thus a lower pumping head is required). Such a tower can, therefore, be accommodated inside a plant room if there is sufficient floor-space and height for exhaust ducting, though roof locations are more common. In the latter cases there is less likelihood of objections by architects or local councils than there might be with taller types of tower.

As height is reduced, so floor area is increased compared with contra-flow. This can be an advantage where the tower is to be carried on the flat roof of a modern building. The distributed load is small and, especially if a deep tank is not essential, the roof may support the tower without need of special reinforcement.

In contra-flow towers the air must pass through the water distribution system, which therefore consists of spray nozzles or a trough and weir system. With the cross-draught tower this is not necessary and a very simplified design is possible. In the Carter "Lo-Line" the water distribution system consists simply of a shallow tank with a perforated base as shown in Fig. 14.

There is an added advantage with this system because one less water

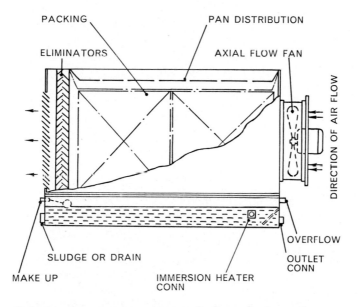

Fig. 12a. Schematic arrangement of forced draught cross-flow tower.

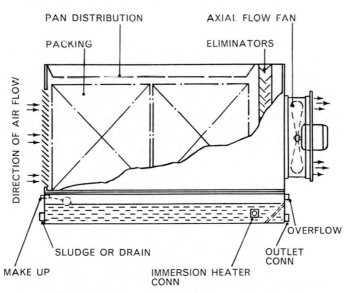

Fig. 12b. Schematic arrangement of induced draught cross-flow tower.

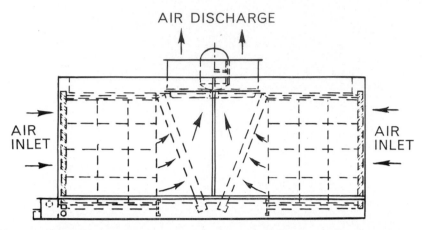

Fig. 13. Schematic arrangement of twinpack induced draught cross-flow tower.

connection is necessary. Hot water is simply directed into the tank by an open ended pipe.

There are also advantages in the design of tower shown in Fig. 13; low air velocities may be used, with therefore lower air resistance, and consequently lower fan hp.

Noise levels are lower and, as comparatively large areas of drift eliminators can be incorporated, there is little risk of "carry-over".

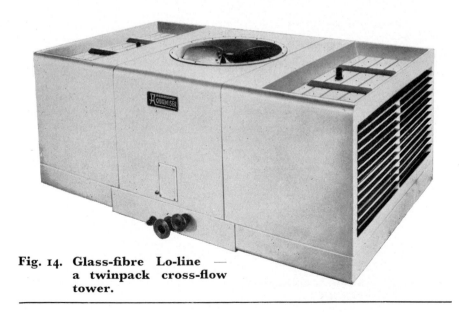

Fig. 14. Glass-fibre Lo-line — a twinpack cross-flow tower.

chapter 3

COOLING TOWER PACKINGS

Splash Packs

Film Packs

Grid Packs

Plate Packs

Materials

3. Cooling Tower Packings

The general principles of cooling tower construction were briefly mentioned in Chapter 2. As explained, the packing is an arrangement inside the tower to increase the rate of heat transfer.

The water to be cooled is allowed to flow over the packing and, in so doing, it presents a large surface area to the airstream.

It is in the packing where most of the cooling takes place. For this reason, it is worthwhile examining in detail the design and construction of the various types.

The *ideal* requirements of any packing are that:-

(a)   It should have a very large surface area for a given volume of material.

(b)   It should be structurally strong.

(c)   It should be chemically inert.

(d)   It should not support scale.

(e)   It should not be susceptible to attack by micro-organisms.

(f)   Its resistance to air flow should be very low.

(g)   Its weight per unit volume should be low.

Regrettably, no packing can comply completely with this 'specification' and in practice the best compromise is arrived at.

COOLING TOWER PACKINGS

There are two main types of packing, defined by the manner in which they produce a large water surface area:-

(1)   Splash Packings.

(2)   Film Packings.

Splash Packings. These types of packing were the first to be widely used and, as the name implies, they rely on splashing to break up the water. They may be as high as 15-20 feet, and a typical arrangement is shown in Fig. 15.

Fig. 15.   Timber splash packing.

As shown, the pack is formed from a number of baffles or laths upon which the falling water impinges, breaking up into numerous small droplets.

Free falling droplets tend to agglomerate and the laths are arranged to continually interrupt this process, creating even smaller droplets. Thus the effectiveness of splash packing depends upon its ability to form these droplets of water.

The rate of cooling also depends to some extent upon the area of wetted surface of the laths. A rectangular cross-section gives the highest surface area for a given volume of material. Wood being rough has a high surface/projected area ratio. Consequently, rectangular section wood laths are frequently used in the construction of splash packings. (Fig. 16a).

A triangular lath (Fig. 16b) is also commonly used, though it requires more material for a given surface area. It has the advantages of being mechanically stronger and presenting less obstruction to air flow whilst still providing a good 'splash' surface to the water.

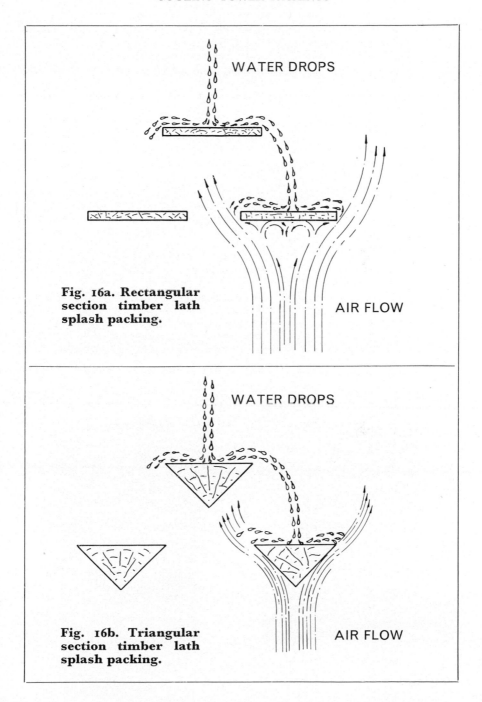

Fig. 16a. Rectangular section timber lath splash packing.

WATER DROPS

AIR FLOW

Fig. 16b. Triangular section timber lath splash packing.

WATER DROPS

AIR FLOW

Splash packings require a comparatively large volume for a given cooling duty and this often results in very high towers.

Because of the formation of very small droplets, there is a danger of water being 'carried-over' with resulting high make-up rates. This necessitates low air-flow rates and, in addition, drift eliminators have to be fitted.

It was to overcome these disadvantages that the film type of packing was developed.

Film Packings. In these types of packing the water forms a large surface area by spreading it in a film. Such packing must have good water/pack adhesive properties, which, with water's low surface tension, ensures that the water forms the thinnest possible film.

With film water flow, relatively high velocities can be used, and the height of the packing dramatically reduced.

Film packings can be divided into three basic types: grid, plate and random.

Grid Packings. These used to be the most commonly used and a typical example is shown in Fig. 17. They consist of a series of grids (usually of timber) arranged in layers, resting upon one another.

The grids are usually constructed from timber strips $1\frac{1}{2}''$ to $2''$ deep by $\frac{3}{8}''$ to $\frac{1}{2}''$ wide. These strips are sometimes serrated to assist water distribution.

The longitudinal members of each layer are arranged crosswise to those in adjacent layers. This arrangement gives good water distribution, and, because of the low resistance to airflow, it is very suitable for natural draught towers.

Fig. 17. Timber grid packing.　　**Fig. 18. Plastic plate packing.**

Such a packing, with unplaned surfaces, will be evenly coated by a continuous water film for flows down to 80 gallons per square foot per hour and can accept flows up to 400 gallons per square foot per hour.

Normal requirements are met, without necessity to employ a mist eliminator, for flows up to 200 gallons per square foot per hour—a feature which arises partly from the unbroken water film on the packing and partly from the special distribution system usually associated with this form of pack. Whilst wood packings have been used with laths at smaller and at larger pitches, 2" pitch is found to be economic for nearly all requirements—most exceptions being for ultra-close approach cooling when the pitch of some of the pack may be closed to 1".

Plate Packings. These were developed to increase, still further, the surface area for a given volume. They also permit the use of high airflow rates.

They consist of thin plates, arranged vertically and closely spaced, each plate being corrugated in some manner. An example of this arrangement is shown in Fig. 18 where the plates are deeply corrugated.

With the most modern thin plastic plate packings, less pack volume and much reduced weight (compared with grid packings) are certain.

Semi-Film Packings. Packings are occasionally encountered in the form of moulded plastic grids in which each member is of T section, thereby combining some splash cooling with some film cooling. For easy cooling duties trays may be separated by 2 to 3 feet instead of being enmeshed closely in true grid (or egg-crate) arrangement. Due to the splashing, all such packs require drift eliminators. It is essential for the water to be entirely clean—also there should be no deposition of organic matter or solids with this type of packing.

Turbulent Flow Packing. One packing, introduced in Sweden and now made under licence for small towers elsewhere, takes the form of a circular mass resembling impregnated honeycombed brown paper with very small holes subject to high water loading. Therefore, very good quality water with no risk of deposition or marine growth etc. is essential.

**Fig. 19.
Random packing.**

Random Packings. In the early days of mechanical draught cooling towers a few packings of the type employed in absorption towers were tried in Chemical and Gas Works eg. with Raschig Rings, but these were never adopted commercially for industry due to excessive air pressure drop, variable cooling performance and the necessity for frequent maintenance and other disadvantages. (Fig. 19).

MATERIALS FOR TOWER PACKINGS

(1) Timber

As previously mentioned, splash and film grid packings are generally made from unplaned timber. Where available, Canadian and American companies use untreated Western Red Cedar or Californian Redwood, but otherwise use other types, suitably treated. European and Russian cooling tower designers originally employed Pitchpine but now all use timber grown in the forests of Northern Sweden, Finland and Nor-Western Russia. Baltic Redwood, also known as Red Deal, easily predominates as a packing material, and for non-structural requirements, though Greenheart, Larch, and a few other woods have been tried for packings, all with less satisfactory results. In India and Pakistan, Chir is generally used for packing. Of all these timbers, preservative impregnated Baltic Redwood is found to be best for the most hazardous parts of a cooling tower. (Although not at present being used, UK-grown Scots Pine would be suitable for the purpose).

The reasons for the superiority of Baltic Redwood are that it is readily available and it can be suitably preservative treated to give high resistance to fungal attack. Also, it has a good natural resistance to chemical degradation from mildly acidic waters. In addition, like other softwoods, it is resistant to delignification of the cellulose in alkaline waters and waters treated with chlorine.

Cooling towers with untreated Pitchpine timber are still in use; there are a number in Britain with shells which are 50 years old. A modern all-timber tower of the best timbers, suitably impregnated, should endure for a similar period, except for the packing, which should last for 30 years, if the treatment is sound.

Due to warmer temperatures, an ample supply of oxygen and high humidities at water distribution and drift eliminator levels, these are the most hazardous parts of a cooling tower. Timber above the water line is subject to attack by both types of wood-destroying fungi, Basidiomycetes, which cause 'wet rot', and the microfungi which cause surface 'soft rot' of timber.

All of the timber within the tower is subject to soft rot attack and timber of small dimensions in which this surface attack assumes importance must be impregnated with higher loadings of preserving salts than, for example, the outer structural timbers, in which attack by the wet rot fungi—less resistant to preservatives than soft rot—is the main hazard.

Some disadvantages of timber packings are:

(a) It breaks down under conditions of high alkalinity or high acidity; alternation of these two conditions being even more adverse.

(b) It provides a material to which algae and other aquatic organisms may readily fasten, although very few such growths use the timber for food.

(c) Packings may require cleaning and the weight and design of timber packings make this extremely difficult. For similar reasons, breakdowns due to chemical or mechanical causes are difficult to repair. However, replacements are cheap and may be installed without the help of the manufacturer.

(d) They can be subject to fungal attack. Fungal decay can be serious, the attack may be one of two main types: Basidiomycete attack, which is further divided into Brown Rot which attacks only the cellulose, and White Rot which attacks both cellulose and lignin. The latter is more prevalent in cooling towers. In the less wet components eg. fan case bearers, the Basidiomycetes group of fungi become the risk if the timber preservation treatment is inadequate.

Soft rot is the worst risk in the packings but is not of serious consequence in the structure. The attacked wood surface becomes darkened and softened, it is then easily rubbed away by attrition of water, or by the fingers. Many species of microscopic fungi, Ascomycetes and Fungi Imperfecti, produce this decay, though Chaetomium Globosum is one of the best known.

Wood preservatives used must be of a type which fix within the wood, i.e. they must react with the wood substance in such a way as to resist subsequent leaching by water. Of these, copper chrome arsenates are a typical example. Creosote, though not so highly fixed, can, nevertheless, at suitably high loadings, give very good protection in structural members.

Decay is usually first noticed in the less wet regions (such as drift eliminators) but may also be occurring in structural members where it is less obvious.

Though timber packings have advantages and are, for some applications, the best choice, the costs of the processing, handling in a saw-mill and, again, in erection on site, are disadvantages.

(2) Asbestos Cement

This has been used in large cooling towers on power stations. Because of the brittle nature of the material it requires careful handling. As its mechanical strength is low and weight comparatively high, the provision of adequate supports presents a problem. This is especially the case where gusts from wind in natural draught towers produce resonance in very large widths of such packing.

However, it is relatively inexpensive, non-inflammable, and not subject to fungal or chemical attack. It may be used in ordinary flat or corrugated sheets, or sheets may be grooved or scarified for low water loadings.

These characteristics make it attractive as a pack material and development work is still proceeding to overcome its shortcomings. Asbestos cement is being used with success for large water distribution troughs and pipes, drift eliminators, air inlet louvres and also for tower cladding.

(3) Ceramics

These have been used as a packing material for many years, particularly in random packs. They do not lend themselves to use in other types and

Fig. 20a.   Results of fungal attack on a timber tower.

Fig. 20b.   Detail of the effects of fungal attack on timber.

because of their relatively high cost they are more used today in absorption or distillation columns where their ability to withstand chemical attack is a distinct advantage.

(4) Metal

Plate packings are frequently formed from metals, as these are easily worked and comparatively cheap. As the materials have a high mechanical strength, quite thin sheet can be used with little external support. Close packing, without obstruction of water or air flow, is possible, with a resulting large surface area for a given volume.

Modern practice has been to use perforated or expanded metal, which, although reducing the area of the plates, actually increases the surface area of the water because of improved water distribution.

Various metals are in use today, the more common are:-

(a) *Aluminium*—when anodised can have a very useful life in average conditions. It should not be used however, in conditions of high alkalinity, or near the sea, where brine laden air can cause severe corrosion. In addition, some water systems contain copper and electrolytic action results, unless effective water treatment is carried out.

(b) *Stainless Steel*—even more expensive than aluminium, but is sometimes used in cooling towers where highly corrosive conditions are combined with high water temperatures. An example of stainless steel packing is shown in Fig. 21. In this particular type of packing, the stainless steel is expanded to reduce weight and cost in addition to improving distribution. This pack has a very high performance and was originally developed by the U.K.A.E.A.

Fig. 21. Stainless steel plate packing.

(c) *Mild Steel*—the cheapest of these metals and is frequently used for that reason. Unfortunately, it corrodes rapidly and therefore, requires treatment before being used in a pack. The most common form of treatment is galvanising which gives fair protection. The zinc in the galvanising can, however, set up an electrolytic action with any copper in the system, particularly if impurities from the air are dissolved in the water, reducing the pH value.

(5) Plastics

Considerable attention has been paid to plastics in recent years because of their many inherent advantages. For example, they can be formed very easily in a variety of shapes, resist chemical attack, are comparatively cheap and often non-inflammable. Expanded plastics, eg: polystyrene, have not met with much success in tower packings. Their main attraction is their ultra light-weight but mechanical strength is poor and there are other disadvantages.

Fig. 22 shows a typical pack, vacuum formed from a grade of PVC chosen for its self-extinguishing characteristics.

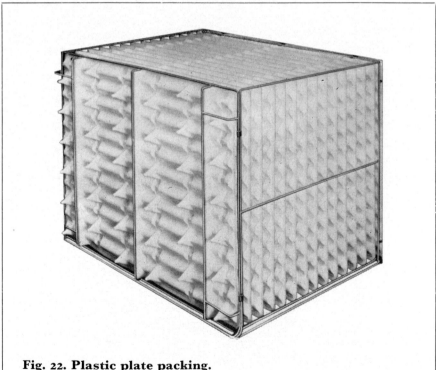

Fig. 22. Plastic plate packing.

The corrugations are arranged to assist even distribution of the water which flows in a film over the plates.

As with other types of pack, a great deal of experience was necessary to determine how best the various materials should be used, and indeed for better materials to be produced.

Those used have included polystyrene, polypropylene, polythene, and polyvinylchloride. All of these are suitable for use in cooling tower packings but are limited to some extent in that they tend to break down at higher water temperatures. They are also susceptible to attack by some organic solvents, though this is rarely of any consequence. However, polythene and polypropylene are sometimes suitable for waters containing aromatic hydrocarbons.

Some of the advantages of plastics have already been mentioned but they are worth enumerating as, undoubtedly, they make plastics most desirable materials for cooling tower use.

(i) The density is low giving a very light, easily supported pack.

(ii) They are inert in any water conditions, acid or alkaline.

(iii) They do not leach away to form a sludge.

(iv) They do not support scale.

(v) They will not support animal or vegetable life.

(vi) They are not subject to electrolytic action.

(vii) They are comparatively cheap.

(viii) They are easily formed.

(ix) They are often non-inflammable.

chapter 4

PRACTICAL ASPECTS OF TOWER SELECTION

4. Practical Aspects of Tower Selection

Let us consider the various factors which need consideration in choosing and siting a cooling tower:—

(1) Determination of Duty

Sometimes, an engineer choosing a cooling tower will have the duty given him by the manufacturer of the equipment being served by the tower.

However, on many occasions an engineer starts his investigation knowing only that a tower is required but not knowing the duty.

He may often have to decide, not only the amount of heat to be dissipated, but the temperature level at which that heat may be dissipated.

To take a common example, there may be existing equipment which is at present being cooled by mains water, and to which it has been decided a cooling tower shall be fitted.

In such a case, the engineer must determine by measurement or calculation the rate at which heat is being rejected to the cooling water.

This is often simple but it can sometimes prove difficult.

If the existing mains flow, inlet and outlet temperatures can be measured then the problem is simple; if not, it might be possible to measure the heat lost by a process fluid being cooled.

In any event, it is important to arrive at a reasonably accurate estimate. Otherwise, obviously, the tower chosen might either be completely inadequate or grossly over-sized.

If the cooling tower is being chosen to serve equipment not yet installed then theoretical investigations are necessary to obtain an accurate estimate of the rate of heat rejection.

The information required by the cooling tower manufacturer is:—

(a) The total heat dissipation rate.

(b) The flow rate of the cooling water.

(c) The desirable water temperature, in summer, to the inlet of the cooling process (i.e. the re-cooled water temperature, in summer, from the tower).

(d)   The design wet bulb temperature (i.e. the summer air wet bulb temperature at which the afore-mentioned duty is to be performed).

Consider these in turn:—

(a) The method of calculating the heat dissipation rate depends upon the process. The difficulty of the calculations involved varies from the simple to the complex.

Fundamentally, there are two different types of calculation. Firstly, there is the case where a solid or liquid is being cooled from a higher temperature to a lower one. Where the lb./hr. of material being cooled, the specific heat and the temperature drop are known the calculation is simple. The rate that heat is rejected to the coolant is given by the following equation:—

$$E = W.s.td.$$

Where:—

   E = Heat dissipation rate in Btu/hr.

   W = Rate of flow of the material being cooled in lb./hr.

   td = Temperature fall of the material being cooled in °F.

   s = Specific heat of the material being cooled in Btu/lb.°F.

(Incidentally a very similar case is that of condensation of a gas to a liquid. Here, the dissipation rate is given by the product of the Latent Heat of Condensation and the flow rate in lb./hr.).

Secondly, there is the type of process where the source of heat is power input, either mechanical or electrical.

In either case, all that is necessary is to find the total power input and convert it to the heat input equivalent.

For example, if some machinery is carrying out an operation on a material, such as grinding or rolling, it is a safe assumption that all the motor h.p. will be converted, ultimately, to heat which will appear in the cooling water. Multiplying the nominal motor horsepower by 2,545 will give the heat dissipation rate in Btu/hr.

If the power input is electrical (as, for example, in an anodising tank) one merely multiplies the power input in kilowatts by 3,415 to obtain the heat dissipation rate in Btu/hr.

It is true that, in both the above examples, not all the power input will ultimately appear in the cooling water. However, it is often very difficult to assess exactly what percentage of the original power input will enter the cooling water. Also, in many practical cases it will be a very high percentage. The methods described will certainly give a conservative figure which will normally leave a reasonable margin of safety, as is usual in heat transfer engineering.

(b) The flow rate of the water is often decided by pressure loss through the equipment being served and the temperature to which the cooling water may rise. For example, with heat exchangers, the lower the water flow and the higher the temperature rise of the coolant, the larger will the heat exchanger need to be. However, the cooling tower will become smaller with increasing temperature range and thus decreasing flow rate. In fact, there is an economic balance, producing an optimum combination of cooling tower and heat exchanger, the detailed treatment of which lies outside the scope of this book.

(c) For a given air wet bulb temperature, the re-cooled water temperature has a considerable effect on tower size. To cool water to the wet bulb temperature of the air would require an infinitely large cooling tower. More practically, as one tries to cool nearer to the air wet bulb temperature the tower size increases very rapidly. It is not usual to have an approach to the air wet bulb temperature of less than 5°F — a more usual figure is 7°F. However, reputable manufacturers will guarantee an approach to within about 3°F of the air wet bulb temperature if this is required.

When selecting a re-cooled water temperature, therefore, choose the highest possible temperature which will permit cooling water to do what is required of it. To do otherwise merely results in the selection of a larger (and therefore more expensive) tower than is necessary.

(d) The choice of the design air wet bulb temperature is of vital importance and needs careful consideration.

There are two main factors in choosing the design air wet bulb temperature:—

1. The meteorological information relevant to the geographical position of the cooling tower site.

2. The results, in the particular equipment being served, if the design air wet bulb temperature is exceeded.

As the highest daytime air wet bulb temperatures recorded in meteorological data sheets refer to only short or peak periods of time, or to temperatures recorded at the same hour each day, it is normally possible to design for a figure less than the highest recorded. The reasons being that (i) temporarily warmer re-cooled water from the cooling tower is quickly lowered in temperature by mixing with the cooling tower pond water, (ii) the thermal lag inherent in the pond, pumping and cooling system compensates for most of the peak time cooling tower performance, when re-cooled water leaving the tower packing may — for minutes only — be higher than desirable. Hence, where a fairly liberal pond capacity is specified, or where high summer conditions may correspond to times of reduced heat dissipation from process plant, or where a small temporary rise in cooling water is acceptable, a design air wet bulb temperature of 5°—10°F below peak temperatures recorded is usually adopted.

The worst embarrassment is probably in air conditioning plant, where, for most "comfort cooling" purposes, it is found necessary to design for the highest air wet bulb temperature encountered on the very few abnormally humid days of the summer in U.K. Cooling towers on similar plants in the tropics may have to be designed for air wet bulb temperatures which are nearer to the peaks recorded.

From the meteorological data for this country given in Table I (over), the average number of hours per annum for which the wet bulb temperature is between certain limits is given, together with a recommended design wet bulb temperature.

TABLE 1

	Average annual number of hours with W.B. Temp Exceeding Certain Limits									
	W.B. Temp (°F)									Recommended Design W.B.
Station	60.0	62.0	64.0	66.0	68.0	70.0	72.0	74.0	76.0	Temp (°F)
Stornoway	64	29	11	3.0	1.0	Nil	Nil	Nil	Nil	61·0
Renfrew (Glasgow)	243	120	50	15	6.0	3.0	1.0	Nil	Nil	64.5
Aldergrove (Ireland)	358	174	78	25	8.0	3.0	Nil	Nil	Nil	65.0
Manchester	410	226	112	51	16	7.0	2.0	1.0	Nil	66.0
Driffield	422	212	89	37	11	2.0	Nil	Nil	Nil	65.0
Elmdon (Birmingham)	449	230	108	46	11	3.0	Nil	Nil	Nil	66.0
Boscombe Down	605	334	176	89	36	10	3.0	Nil	Nil	67.0
Lympne	757	416	197	83	39	13	4.0	2.0	Nil	67.5
Croydon	381	188	92	39	13	4.0	1.0	Nil	Nil	65.5
Pembroke Dock	579	264	132	53	18	10	3.0	1.0	Nil	66.5

If the operating air wet bulb temperature rises above the design air wet bulb temperature, the temperature of the water leaving the cooling tower will rise above the design temperature, but not as much as the amount by which the operating air wet bulb temperature exceeds the design air wet bulb temperature.

The design temperature has to be decided for each case on its merits and only after careful consideration of the points discussed above.

To illustrate the effect of wet bulb temperature on tower performance, the graph in Fig. 23 shows the results of wet bulb temperature variation

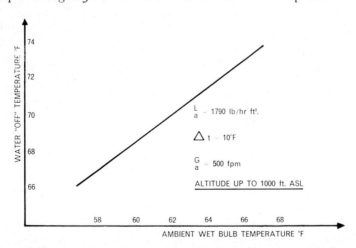

Fig. 23. Typical contra-flow pack. Variation in re-cooled temperature with varying wet bulb temperatures.

on a specific tower. Here, for constant water flow rate, air flow rate and temperature range, the variation in water-off temperatures with wet bulb temperature is given.

(2) Capital v Running Costs

It is generally true to say, that for a given cooling duty, for the same type of cooling tower, one has the choice between a relatively large tower, with low fan power consumption, and on the other hand, a relatively small tower with large fan power consumption. Also, one can make a completely valid choice of tower between these two extremes. In any tower comparison of economic costs, note should be taken of the head from the cold water pond to the warm water inlet pipe, as this permits pumping costs to be included in the assessment.

Theoretically, there is a choice of tower, somewhere between the two extremes, that gives optimum economy. That is to say, a tower for which the combined capital and running cost is a minimum over the period during which the tower is to be "written off".

However, practical considerations often preclude the choice of a cooling tower merely on the ground of optimum economy. For example, the space available for a tower may force the choice of a compact tower with a relatively large fan power.

Furthermore, it should be borne in mind that the space occupied by a cooling tower has a value which is often considerable, and strictly, site value and foundation and pond basin costs should be included in the cost of the tower when making any choice of the optimum size.

The cooling tower very soon offsets its initial cost by reducing water consumption. In fact, most installations pay for themselves in less than 5 years and in some cases only one year. Take, as an example, an actual case where a furnace with water cooled walls required water at the rate of 1,250 gph. A certain amount of pipework, including a pump, was installed with the furnace, but this was redesigned and extended to allow for re-circulation in the cooling tower.

The comparison of costs was as follows:—

System Running Mains Water to Waste		System Recirculating Cooling Water Through a Cooling Tower	
Capital Costs		*Additional Capital Costs*	
Pipework, etc.	£100	Pipework, etc.	£950
		Cooling Tower	£300
Pump and necessary wiring	£25	Pump and necessary wiring for pump and cooling tower fan	£50
TOTAL	£125	TOTAL	£1,300

Running Costs (2,000 hr/year)		*Running Costs* (2,000 hr/year)	
Water @ 2/6 per 1,000 gal.	£312	Make-up water	£13
Electricity @ 2d. per kw./hr.	£5	De-sludging	£13
Maintenance	£10	Pump and Cooling tower fan	£50
TOTAL	£327	TOTAL	£76

Time required to offset additional installation costs:—

$$\frac{1300 \quad - \quad 125}{327 \quad - \quad 76} = 4.77 \text{ years}$$

In this example, the tower would pay for itself in less than 5 years, and this, as it happens, is not a favourable example. The tower used was of all-plastic construction with a glass fibre casing and PVC packing. In addition, the water was cooled through 40°F (unusually high in practice), resulting in a high water loss due to evaporation.

(3) Effect of Altitude

Special consideration must be given when the site is at any appreciable altitude above sea level.

The greatest effect of altitude is that the mass of air delivered by the fan is reduced. This is due to the reduction in density combined with the fact that a fan is essentially a constant volume machine.

The tower is designed on mass flow of air per unit horizontal cross-sectional area of pack and care must be taken, therefore, when selecting the fan. In other words, a tower selected for a duty at sea level, might be incapable of meeting that duty at a higher altitude.

The other factor is that as altitude increases, air at a given temperature is capable of holding a larger amount of water vapour. This tends to offset the density factor, but its effect is comparatively small particularly at low water temperature levels.

(4) Choice of Site

The available site can often determine the type of tower to be used, or occasionally the type of tower necessary can determine the site.

In practice the engineer assesses the possible sites he might use, the types of tower available, and then makes a judgment which depends upon various factors:—

(a) *The convenience in running pipes and placing pumps to circulate the cooling water.*

A common difficulty occurs when a user places a tower below the level of a cooling system with a large capacity. When the pump is switched off, the system empties into the tower sump and valuable water is lost down the overflow.

To avoid this trouble one of several precautions can be taken:—

(1)   The tower can be put on the same level as the system.

(2)   The tower pond can be made large enough to take the drain-back.

(3)   Non-return valves can be fitted in the water lines.

(b) *The load-bearing capacity of the surface on which the tower is to be placed.*

If a tower is to be mounted on a roof, a cross-draught, low-silhouette tower (with large plan area) might be needed to limit the load on the roof.

It should be remembered that the operating weight, (i.e. including water in the distribution system, packing and tank) should be used when making roof stress calculations.

(c) *The necessity to limit interference with airflow, both to and from the cooling tower.*

Such interference may take the form of a restriction to airflow into the tower, which might happen if the tower is placed with the air intakes too near a wall.

Another form of interference is recirculation, which occurs when the air discharged from the tower is deflected towards the air inlets and therefore drawn into the tower again. This, of course, raises the wet bulb temperature of the inlet air, reducing tower performance.

If the obstruction is nearer than a distance corresponding to 150% of the air inlet height there are definite possibilities of excessive air inlet resistance, insufficient air supply, and increased noise level. In practice, it is best to work to a minimum distance 200% of the air inlet height, if possible. The effect of obstructive walls on both incoming and outgoing air is more serious in a forced draught cooling tower.

Care should be taken to avoid siting the tower near hot air or gas discharge points, such as ventilation outlets, boiler flues, etc. As before, the effect is to raise wet bulb temperature at the tower air intake, with a consequent loss of performance.

(d) *Whether the tower must be sited indoors.*

If this is necessary due to site restrictions, it is essential to duct the outlet from the tower through the roof or wall of the building. It is not always necessary to duct fresh air to the tower inlet, as when conditions permit, large louvres can be placed in an adjacent wall.

In these conditions, the layout of the forced draught tower makes it a very convenient choice. Figs. 24a and 24b show the way in which this type of tower can be used to give a very compact arrangement.

(e) The permissible operating noise level of the tower.

Obviously this can vary greatly depending upon the application and type of tower used, and in fact, the necessity to limit noise can be a major factor in deciding tower type and position.

If the type of tower to be used is dictated by other factors, the engineer can only position it as far as possible away from noise sensitive areas, or fit expensive silencers. Alternatively, if the tower must be sited near such areas, its size may have to be increased to keep down air pressure drop and consequently, fan noise level.

Though the noise level of a cooling tower is often of only minor consequence in industrial cooling applications, it can be of major importance where the tower is sited near residential or office buildings.

For this reason noise from cooling towers is dealt with in rather more detail in the next chapter.

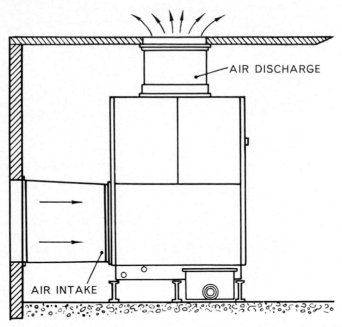

Fig. 24a. Induced draught contra-flow tower sited within a building.

(5) Appearance

Only since about 1950 have purchasers begun to insist on cooling towers of appearance compatible with elevations of adjacent plant and buildings. Even now, several suppliers offer towers which are only a negligible improvement on the unsightly towers of pre-war years. Since Industry and

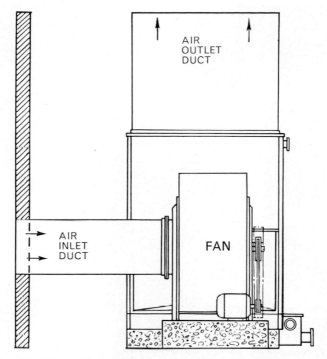

Fig. 24b. Forced draught contra-flow tower sited within a building.

Town Planning Authorities in most parts of the U.K. now very properly pay much more attention than hitherto to shape, proportions, material and colour of installations, a purchaser should satisfy himself that the shell of the cooling tower offered to him will, in fact, present a satisfactory appearance for many years ahead.

The old timber cooling tower had a single skin, an exposed and inelegant structural framework, unsightly blemishes from water leakages and a depressing aspect from the use of creosote for timber preservation. All of these disadvantages are to be condemned today. Modern advances in shell design and appearance can result in a cooling tower being an architectural feature of quality, taking its place as a prominent but compatible edifice among a group of industrial or commercial structures. Alternatively, the modern tower can often be rendered quite inconspicuous, beyond criticism by owners or nearby residents.

Two large multi-cell cross-draught cooling towers.

Courtesy of Film Cooling Towers (1925) Ltd.

chapter 5

NOISE FROM COOLING TOWERS

5. Noise from Cooling Towers

There is an ever-increasing demand to restrict the use of equipment which generates offensive noise. This is a factor to which more and more attention must be paid, particularly in mixed residential, commercial and industrial areas where the general noise climate is worsening by 1 to 2 dB per year.

Failure to obtain information on the noise level of a proposed cooling tower, or failure to realise the significance of data on noise levels given by manufacturers, sometimes results in engineers installing a cooling tower which causes a considerable noise nuisance.

Noise from a cooling tower can be caused by:

(a) The movement of the impeller of the fan.

(b) Movement of air through the tower.

(c) Bearing noise from fan, motor and gearbox.

(d) Magnetic hum.

(e) Movement of water through the tower.

Each of these is described below:

(a) The movement of the impeller of the fan

Noise here emanates from the swirl of air as it changes velocity and direction. The most objectionable noise comes from a high speed fan having the minimum number of blades, which for axial flow fan is, of course, only two blades.

High speed fans are of smaller diameters than would otherwise be the case and for this reason are generally cheaper. A compromise has to be found wherein an economic fan can perform satisfactorily (a) without creating excessive pulsating on the fan casing and (b) without creating excessive high frequency noise from a sudden change of air movement at the blade tips.

In a carefully designed cooling tower there should be no obstruction near the fans in the air stream of size or proximity likely to create turbulence and consequently additional noise. This requires careful design of fan bearers and safety mesh supports, etc.

(b) Movement of Air through the Tower

If the packing is fed from troughs and the water distribution level has numerous bearers and platforms, air disturbance caused by them may add a little low frequency noise.

In the packing, air movement generates very little noise. More noise, of course, is produced where the free areas are small or where air is moved through the packing at comparatively high velocities.

(c) Bearing noise from fan, motor and gearbox

These are common origins of mechanical noise. Ball and roller bearings today give very long life without excessive noise. However, specially large bearings can sometimes be supplied (also, sleeve bearings) to secure minimum noise.

Reduction gears are now invariably multi-start, high efficiency worm-type gears. Reputable makers use liberal dimensions, thus, where maintenance, inspection and lubrication are not neglected, a very long life and an absence of disturbing noise can be assured. A badly aligned drive or a worn ball bearing can soon produce an objectionable rumble and the noise nuisance is worse on fans fitted to forced draught cooling towers.

There are still a number of old towers using chain drives or bevel gear drives and sometimes suppliers offer these reduction systems on new towers. This is poor practice. Both methods of power transmission introduce noise, apart from such equipment having a relatively short life.

(d) Magnetic Hum

All motors — like other electrical plant possessing windings in laminated steel cores — produce 50 Hz hum with minor harmonics. Motors built to BSS and supplied from reputable sources have designs with flux densities, core clamps and other details which usually keep hum to an acceptable low level. Most cooling tower fan noise has only a small component attributable to magnetic hum which may usually be ignored. However, it may become of consequence when designing cooling towers with very quiet centrifugal fans when supersilent motors are sometimes necessary.

(e) Movement of Water through the Tower

Some hiss is often noticeable within a tower where spray distribution is used. In splash packings, noise is heard from the impingement of water streams on the splash laths. All other plastic and timber packings are virtually silent in use. From the bottom of the packing, however, water drops to the basin and this can produce nearly all the hiss heard from some cooling towers. A large tower, designed with very high air inlets, or a tower designed for high water loading per square foot of packing will be noisier than average. Only very rarely will it be found necessary to reduce this noise. If necessary, the cooling tower manufacturer can provide a 'splash deck' spanning the tower a very few inches above the water surface. On this 'splash deck' descending water glides over inclined slats to enter the basin with a small final drop and consequently much reduced noise. On small towers a layer of foam rubber supported by a frame has been used.

Noise Measurement

Sound is pressure energy and can only be measured as such. The instrument used is a sound level meter consisting of a microphone which converts the pressure energy to electrical energy and feeds it, via an amplifier to a voltmeter calibrated in decibels.

The decibel (dB) is the unit of sound measurement and indicates the sound pressure level (SPL) above a reference level of 0·0002 microbar. Because the range of pressure levels is so great, a direct scale would be inconveniently large and so the decibel scale is a logarithmic one. In practice, a value in decibels is only a useful indication of subjective noise level if one has an idea of the levels of some typical sounds. Table 12 on page 181, will perhaps be helpful. The dB ratings given there are on the 'A' scale.

Industrial sound level meters are usually capable of recording 'overall' sound pressure levels on three scales, namely A, B and C. The 'C' scale gives virtually uniform response over the whole frequency range and within the limits of accuracy of the instrument, gives the true sound pressure level. The 'A' scale and the 'B' scale settings on the instrument modify the scale reading to give values more indicative of the response of the human ear, which is not constant over the whole frequency range.

More complex sound level meters are capable of breaking down the overall sound pressure level within the range of frequencies indicated. The frequency band-widths are identified by the mid-frequency of each band. In the U.K., these are:— 63, 125, 250, 500, 1000, 2000, 4000 and 8000 Hz. When the sound pressure levels within each band are measured and plotted as a curve this is called a 'frequency analysis'. If the individual levels are added together logarithmically the sum will approximate to the overall sound pressure level. Because the 'C' scale gives a close indication of actual overall pressure levels, and can be analysed mathematically many engineers prefer to use it, especially when considering a frequency analysis or plotting a noise criteria value (see below). However, the 'Wilson Report' on Noise (Command 2056, HMSO), published in 1963, deals exclusively in overall 'A' scale values (dBA). In addition, BS.4485 part 2 (Water Cooling Towers — Methods of test and acceptance testing) stipulates that cooling tower noise shall be measured in dBA. Therefore, it is likely that dBC values will gradually cease to be used in cooling tower work, except for air conditioning purposes, where noise level criteria curves are likely to remain popular. Sound power level (dBW) cannot be measured directly, but some manufacturers give sound data in terms of power values. The reference level for power is 10^{-12} watts and it is numerically equal to pressure level measured at zero distance from the noise source.

The effect of Distance

Sound power levels are independent of distance. Free field sound pressure levels, however, reduce with distance from the source and Fig. 25 shows how this occurs. If x is the distance of the microphone from the sound source, at which the noise level is, say, 80 dBC, then 10x is 10 times this distance, at which the noise level would be only 60 dBC. Any free field sound pressure level figure is meaningless unless the distance at which it was measured is also given.

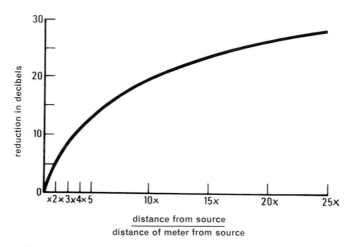

distance from source
distance of meter from source

Fig. 25. Graph showing relation between sound reduction and distance from a point source of noise

Addition of Noise Levels

Quantities in decibels can only be added logarithmically. For example, 80 dBC+80 dBC=83 dBC. Table 2 shows how to add noises at different levels.

TABLE 2   Addition of Noise Levels

Difference between the two levels to be combined dB	0	1	2	4	6	9
Number of dB to be added to higher level to obtain combined level	3	$2\frac{1}{2}$	2	$1\frac{1}{2}$	1	$\frac{1}{2}$

Noise Criteria Curves

The human ear, when reacting to sounds, takes into account not only their pressure level but also their frequency or pitch. Thus, although the ear responds to all frequencies between about 25 and 15,000 Hz. it is less sensitive to the lower frequencies. Not only this, but in general, there is less tolerance of high frequency sounds. A method of noise evaluation which takes this into account is the use of NOISE CRITERIA CURVES, these are shown in Fig. 26.

Noise criteria curves each indicate equal human tolerance over the usual frequency range. They have been drawn up from extensive experiments with human subjects. Each curve is identified by a number which coincides with the noise pressure level in the 2,000 Hz. octave band. The lower the NC rating of a cooling tower, the quieter and more acceptable it will be.

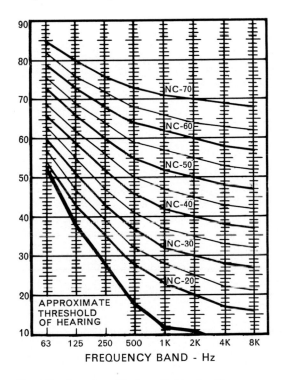

Fig. 26. Graph showing Noise Criteria Curves.

Environmental Noise Level

This is a very difficult subject upon which to reach conclusions, since noise is subjective and each individual has his own idea of what is a nuisance. The criterion in laying down equipment noise levels should ideally be to achieve a noise climate which will not cause disturbance *at all*, having regard to the environment. This is rarely possible without a lot of space and a lot of money being available and, it is more usual to specify noise levels which will merely avoid action being taken under the Noise Abatement Act.

Under Section 1 of the Act, noise which is a nuisance becomes a statutory nuisance and, in general, subject to the power of the Public Health Department of the local authority, to prevent the nuisance from continuing. Indeed, the local authority has a duty to exercise this power. This they do mainly by persuasion and advice, although they can bring proceedings in a Magistrates Court for the enforcement of an abatement notice. A fine and a continuing daily penalty are the result of ignoring this. If work could be carried out to reduce the noise to a satisfactory level, and the offending firm is reluctant to do this, the local authority also has power to carry out such work as is required and then charge the offender the full cost.

Alternatively, three or more persons who, as occupiers of land or premises, are aggrieved by the noise nuisance, may start proceedings under the Act. Noise can also be the subject of a civil action under Common Law if it continually interferes with health, comfort or convenience 'according to plain and sober and simple notions obtaining among English people'. Only one aggrieved person is needed for this.

Under the Noise Abatement Act, it is a defence for the offender to prove that he has taken the "best practicable means" to prevent or counteract the noise, having regard to cost and local conditions and circumstances. This defence does not apply under Common Law. It is also no answer to say that the cause of the noise is the exercise of a business or trade in a proper manner.

How then, to avoid this unpleasant legal action? The answer is to choose equipment which suits the noise climate of the environment.

In certain spheres of activity, there may be some guidance. The Ministry of Health, for instance, have the standards indicated in Table 4, applicable to hospital installations. (Notice that in this table the frequency bands are identified in accordance with practice in the U.S.A.).

In Birmingham, the Public Health Authority stipulates that no new equipment shall have a noise level greater than NC 30 measured at the boundary of the land in which the equipment is installed. (The inference is that they would not uphold a nuisance complaint if the equipment rating were below this). However, if there were offices or conference rooms nearer than the nearest boundary, even NC 30 might be too high. The 'Wilson Report' tentatively suggests that noise level inside living rooms and bedrooms, should not exceed the figures given in Table 3 for more than ten per cent of the time.

TABLE 3   Recommended Neighbourhood Noise Levels (dBA)

Situation	Day	Night
Country areas	40 dBA	30 dBA
Suburban areas, away from main traffic routes ...	40 dBA	35 dBA
Busy urban areas...	50 dBA	35 dBA

TABLE 4   Recommended Hospital Noise Levels (dBC)

Recommended maximum average sound pressure levels for machines with dimensions of 6 ft. or more.

Sound pressure levels are to be measured at 6 feet from each machine in at least five positions on each side and above and below (if machine does not site on floor). Readings shall be averaged arithmetically, except that all readings more than 10 decibels below the maximum reading shall be disregarded in taking the average.

Sound pressure level re 0.0002 microbar

Frequency band, Hz.

	20–75	75–150	150–300	300–600	600–1200	1200–2400	2400–4800	4800–9600
Schedule II	58	50	42	36	32	30	30	30
Schedule IV	95	90	86	82	89	77	77	77

If hospital rooms do not have acoustical treatment of $\frac{3}{4}$ in. tile or equivalent on ceiling, subtract 8 decibels from all maximum sound levels.

Sound rating schedule for predominant hospital noise sources

Schedule No.		Noise Source
II	Lift, corridor.[2] Mechanical roof-type fans— Mechanical roof-type extract fan with ductwork to toilets. Transformers—(50 feet from building) Transformers—(within building) Ventilation, grille (corridor)	(1 foot from intake)

(6 feet from grille) |
| IV | Boiler house equipment.[3] Lift room equipment. Ventilation, plant-room. | |

MINISTRY OF HEALTH NOTES

1. Preferred I.S.O. frequencies in cycles per second for acoustical measurements and for geometric frequencies of band-pass filters are:— 16-31.5-63-125-500-1000-2000-4000-8000-16,000. The British Standards which refer are as follows:—

    B.S. 3493:1963   Preferred frequencies for acoustical measurements.

    B.S. 2475:1964   Octave and one-third octave band-pass filters.

2. The sound measurement should be taken 6 ft. from lift doors.

3. The sound measurement should be taken 12 ft. from equipment in open air or anechoic chamber.

    (Extracted from Hospital Design Note—Noise Control)
    (HMSO—SO Code No. 32–520–4).

Table 5 Acceptable neighbourhood NC Levels

Dwellings In:	Daytime only	Evenings	All Night
Rural area	NC 30	NC 25	NC 20
Suburban area	NC 35	NC 30	NC 25
Urban, residential	NC 40	NC 35	NC 30
Commercial area	NC 45	NC 40	NC 35
Industrial area	NC 50	NC 45	NC 40

(Extracted from: Design for Sound, VW.307 Jan. 68, Woods Fans Ltd., Colchester).

For some years the figures in Table 5 have also been used by some fan manufacturers.

Low Noise Level Cooling Towers

For some applications, it is necessary to supply cooling towers with noise levels lower than usual. Invariably the result of designing a tower so that it has a reduced noise level is to increase the price. However, it is far cheaper to accept that a quiet cooling tower is necessary from the start than to attempt to remedy the situation after an excessively noisy tower has been installed.

There are various ways in which towers can be designed so as to produce lower noise levels, for example:

(i)   to derate the tower.

(ii)   to fit silencers.

(iii)   to use two speed motors.

(iv)   to use centrifugal fans.

Each of these is described below:

(i) derating the tower

By selecting a tower which is physically oversized for the cooling load, but with a correspondingly lower air speed, a slow speed fan can be fitted. This has the added bonus of greatly reduced fan power. It is, however, an inefficient and costly method of noise reduction.

(ii) fitting silencers

So called silencers (actually, noise attenuators is the proper term) are a practicable means of noise reduction on small towers where their size and weight does not impose excessive strain on the tower shell. Straight-through silencers are the simplest but the degree of attenuation is slight, whereas pod-type silencers give much better attenuation but impose a pressure loss and usually require bigger fan motors.

The cost, weight and height of silencers, increase very rapidly with diameter and they are not often a successful form of attenuation for larger fans. Of course, if noise emission from the air inlets is also a problem, inlet silencers would be a much more difficult and costly proposition.

(iii) **using two speed motors**

If a lower noise level is required at times when there is also a reduction in cooling load, for example, during the night, then two speed motors can be used. They are relatively inexpensive, also reduce fan power at low speed and can be automatically controlled.

(iv) **using centrifugal fans**

The most effective noise reduction is obtained by designing the tower using centrifugal fans. For small to medium towers, it is also relatively inexpensive, although it can double the area occupied by the tower. Centrifugal fans are inherently quieter for comparable duties and although bulky, they are often the only practical solution if really low NC ratings are required.

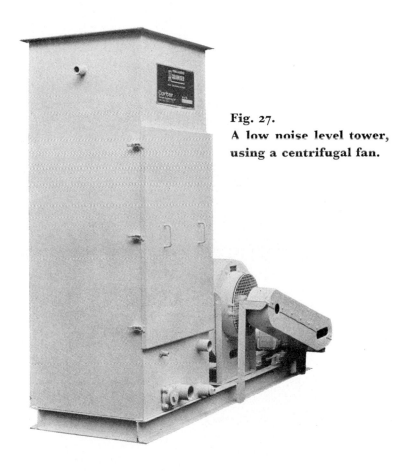

Fig. 27.
A low noise level tower,
using a centrifugal fan.

The cost of attenuated towers

In a theoretical investigation for a proposed twin-cell installation in the South of England, the following figures in Table 6 were obtained. Although precise costs will vary with tower size, of course, the relationship between the methods of attenuation discussed will be similar for all tower sizes.

TABLE 6   The effectiveness of various Noise Reduction Methods

Arrangement	Effectiveness	Cost
Axial flow fans ...　...　...　...　...	below NC 70	100%
Straight through silencers　...　...　...	below NC 60	130%
Derated axial flow fans　...　...　...	below NC 55	170%
Two speed motors　...　...　...　...	below NC 55	135%
Pod-type silencers　...　...　...　...	below NC 40	150%
Centrifugal fans　...　...　...　...	below NC 30	140%

Noise Level Reduction on Site

What can be done if an installed cooling tower proves too noisy? Obviously this will depend upon how noisy it is and upon site circumstances. The action taken should be effective and the cost as low as possible.

Often it is possible to accept a slightly higher recooled water temperature than that specified. Also, the maximum cooling capacity can sometimes be found to exceed the required cooling duty by a considerable amount. Either or both of these considerations may reveal that the tower can be derated by reducing the airspeed and a lower fan r.p.m. can be used. (This would involve a change of electric motor or a rewind of the original motor if the impeller were directly driven).

If the resultant noise level is still not low enough, sound baffling may now be considered. This can take the form of extra sound absorbent cladding to the tower or sound baffling walls enclosing the tower. The attenuation provided is very difficult to predict but Fig. 28 shows the result achieved on a twin cell tower using extra sound absorbent cladding.

If the noise level is still not low enough, then silencers may be considered, provided the tower's fan deck is strong enough (or can be reinforced) to take the weight. Often, only pod-type silencers are sufficiently effective. Unfortunately a more powerful fan motor may need to be fitted. If the tower were excessively noisy or if the stipulated noise level were clearly beyond the capability of a pod-type silencer, then the tower would have to be dismantled and rebuilt using a centrifugal fan. If this were done to the towers illustrated in Fig. 29, then the cost of converting from curve (a) to curve (e) would be about 225% of the curve (a) cost. (Compared with only 140% for using this arrangement in the first instance).

The lesson to be learned is that the noise problem should be fully investigated before a tower is ordered. Considerations such as noise reflection, reverberation, vibration and diffraction should be referred to experts.

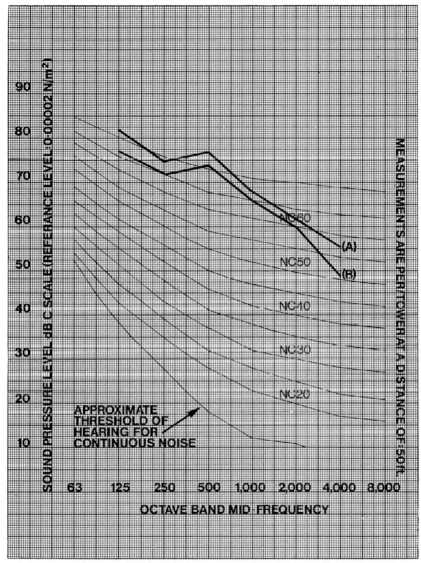

Fig. 28.

(A) Tower with no sound insulation.

(B) Tower with sound insulation as illustration left. Tower has fibrous baffling material around upper shell and fans. Plywood set off inlet louvres but no insulation.

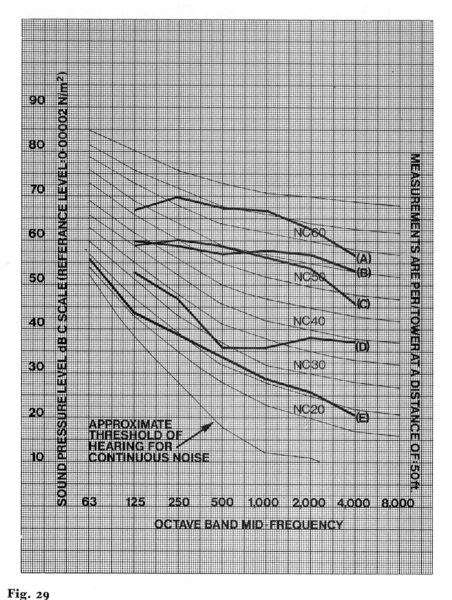

Fig. 29
(A) Axial Flow Fans. (B) Straight Through Silencers. (Ci) Derated
Tower. (Cii) Axial Flow Fans at $\frac{3}{4}$ speed. (D) Pod Type Silencers.
(E) Centrifugal Fans.

chapter 6

MAINTENANCE

> Electro-Mechanical Equipment
> Packing
> Distribution System
> Shell/Structure
> Pond Basins

---

6. Maintenance

Water cooling towers are structures in which, in most cases, access to the inside is impracticable for most of the year. Towers in steelworks, gasworks and power stations may be in continuous use for two or three years. It follows that towers should be designed to ensure efficient cooling for a minimum of upkeep and work. Nevertheless, no item of capital plant can function indefinitely without maintenance and, as with a machine, a cooling tower's life and certainly its performance is maintained by short, though regular, inspection.

Suppliers differ in their recommendations as to frequency of inspections. Natural draught towers do not normally justify inspections more than once every three or four months. Mechanical draught towers, dependent upon single fans, should be visited perhaps once per month, and a multi-cell tower needs inspection at average intervals of six weeks. The following are particular points to be noted.

Electro-Mechanical Equipment

(i) *Gears*

Gearboxes on indirectly driven fans need the most strict inspection. Being totally enclosed in order to operate permanently in a saturated atmosphere, cooling tower gearboxes have an exceptionally high reliability providing worm loading and tooth rubbing speeds are not excessive for the metals employed. However, it is essential to check the oil bath never falls below the minimum safe level, leakages at bearings not being tolerated. The bearings, of course, are of great importance and for the larger gear drives specialist bearing advice may be obtained from the cooling tower supplier. It is advisable to check gearbox oil and bearing temperature if wear is suspected. If rain-water or condensate is feared to be mixed with gearbox oil, and, at all events, at the manufacturers' prescribed periods, all oil should be drained and replenished.

(ii) *Power transmissions*

The couplings and transmission shafting on indirectly driven fans are normally assembled together and are designed to accommodate a considerable degree of misalignment. Metal finish may be of a proprietary enamel but if rusting develops it is not usually necessary to take corrective measures. It is advisable for non-metallic cushions on couplings to be renewed every 3-5 years, though a longer life is common. Some, but not many, flexible couplings require periodic lubrication.

Bearer fixings need regular inspection for tightness.

(iii) *Motors*

Motors on cooling tower fans are almost invariably brushless and without slip rings or commutators, hence they need less service than any other motor. Inspection should verify that the feet are secure, that the fan casing does not foul the shaft and that the end cap and coupling are protected to obviate risk of injury to someone standing near. Bearings on modern motors are normally ball and roller type, needing no lubricant in most cases. Bearing changes at intervals of 5-7 years might be anticipated, depending on fan usage.

In a hot climate it is generally wise to place a detachable sheet steel shade over the whole of the motor frame, leaving a gap of 4 in. minimum between the motor and its shade.

(iv) *Starters*

Motor starters may be of various types. If out of doors, they should be either on the fan deck or should be supplemented by isolating switches immediately adjoining the motors. Starters, Controllers or Switches, if designed for outdoor duty, need negligible servicing — generally, annual inspections, will suffice. It is, of course, important that only competent electricians be permitted to set overload trips and replace fuses. In tropical countries there is sometimes a risk of termites building up short-circuit shunts after ingress through very small apertures in conduit, drain holes, etc. Where circuit breakers are of oil-immersed patterns or fitted with oil dashpots it is vital that only the specified oils should be employed and no other oils. Contactors or switches for two-speed fan motors require more frequent inspection and periodic cleaning, adjustment or renewal of contact tips, but such work is generally specified in separate switch manufacturers' maintenance instructions. Where an oil immersed transformer is provided, either for auto-transformer starting or for supplying a battery of fan motors, this should be inspected quarterly, checks being made on insulating oil level in conservator tank or core tank and the state of the de-hydrating breather observed, if fitted. It is recommended that all such transformers should have primary and secondary cable or conduit boxes but where there are exposed bushings in sandy or dusty localities, it may be necessary to shut down the plant at appropriate times for bushing cleaning to remove danger of flashover.

(v) *Fans*

Fans are carefully balanced at Works and it is essential that they remain accurately balanced at all times. A fan can be out of balance if a detachable blade has been set at a wrong pitch angle, but the more likely hazard is unbalance due to mechanical damage of an impeller, or accumulation of uneven chemical deposits on the blades, or damage and dislocation of any blade covering. There have been cases where large, inquisitive birds have dived upon a glistening fan and, though meeting death, have damaged the impellers upon impact, thereby creating unbalance and producing bearing trouble. A light encrustation of salt on a blade is of no consequence but large deposits of salt precipitated from brackish water, or deposits from chemically treated waters, should be carefully wiped off as occasion demands — certainly often enough to prevent a thick build-up on an impeller. If a hardwood blade is covered by a protective skin of glass fibre, plastic or rubber material, or if a leading edge of a blade is protected by a stainless steel strip, these need occasional examination for looseness of fixing adhesive or pins. Fans with looseness at these points are potentially dangerous.

No-one must risk work on a fan unless he is in personal control of an Isolator, Main Switch or Starter.

(vi) *Vibration Switches*

Most vibration switches seem to be tied up in practice. Where they are in use and effective they need quarterly inspection to ensure freedom from dirt and water.

(vii) *Lighting*

Many fan decks of induced draught towers have fixed lamps and inspecl tion lamp outlets. Supports, wiring, switches and fittings need annua- inspection for security where subject to vibration. These items also need an annual insulation test where wiring is unprotected.

Small-duty induced draught contra-flow tower, demonstrating ease of pack removal.

73

(viii) *Guards*

Most fans have metal guards and occasionally these guards sag, rust, or become loose from vibration. A loose guard which can foul a fan impeller is highly dangerous. All guards should be kept in tight condition and on no account should fans be allowed to operate without guards if they have been removed for some reason. It is best that guards be well protected against corrosion and that fixings and bearers be of liberal size to withstand vibration.

Packing

The numerous types of cooling tower packing on the market are characterised by widely differing claims as to maintenance requirements. Suppliers' recommendations should be sought and followed but these observations may be a general guide where information is not obtainable or is mislaid.

(i) *Wood*

Timber packing, like other packing, must be free of scale. If water is hard and throws out its hardness salts in the packing, cooling will suffer, process plant will be less efficient and packing may collapse from weight of deposits. The solution in such cases does not lie with packing maintenance but with water treatment. Packing which is heavily fouled from hardness scale generally requires replacement.

Wood packing may be subject to fungal attack, in which case the worst decay is likely to be in the upper layers of packing. The services of Timber Preservative Specialists should be invited if decay is in its early stage — otherwise the only remedy, where decay is advanced and the structural failure of packing seems probable, is to replace the packing.

The effect of a scale-fouled packing is probably worse with a film grid pack. The effect of a decayed pack is often more pronounced with a splash type packing of the aris lath type.

If a cooling tower is put out of action for some weeks the wood packing, (also drift eliminator and the internal structural bracings of the shell) will dry out and shrink in size. Repeated drying and wetting of wood in towers with "on"-"off" duty cycles precipitates surface cracking and the onset of degradation of the wood. In such towers, therefore, a tarpaulin should be drawn across the fan casing(s) for induced draught towers or drawn across the exhaust aperture for forced draught towers, to ensure shade below. Also, if possible, the circulating water pumps (or a hose) should be run for a few minutes each week to dampen the wood surfaces. This procedure is particularly advisable in towers in tropical localities.

(ii) *Plastic*

With the exception of the very few expanded polystyrene packings it is true to assert that all plastic packings are potentially more trouble-free than all other packings but inspection should quickly reveal if there is deformation due to high water temperatures, detritus inclusions, or shift or collapse of packing supports or packing spacers. In the event of major movement of the packing it should be cleaned and refixed at a suitable opportunity; minor obstructions can generally be left.

Module of lightweight plastic plate packing. Easily handled by one man without the aid of lifting tackle.

(iii) *Cement Asbestos*

Providing the sheets have been handled and placed into position without cracking, these should endure for a very long time without need for maintenance.

Cement asbestos sheets, however, can crack and break up readily if subject to much icing in winter and they can quickly deform or change position if bearers and spacers are not liberally designed to withstand the weight and the vibration of packing under natural or induced draught. Scale will adhere easily to cement asbestos packing but such packing is not subject to fungal attack.

If a cement asbestos packing is in good shape after its first twelve months use, it should only be necessary to inspect the packing thereafter once or twice a year.

(iv) *Algae and Slime*

These hazards will receive comment in Chapter 7. Extensive development of slime and algae can lead to a noticeable lowering in cooling efficiency in summer and, in consequence, summer inspections of packing should determine whether or not fouling from these causes is bad enough to merit some remedy. Trays or grids which are two or three feet apart may be easily removed for cleaning and replacement. However, as fouling is worse in summer, and it is in summer when most towers cannot be taken out of service, it is the provision of a suitable algaecide or slime deterrent treatment by specialists, rather than service by Cooling Tower builders or Works maintenance men that forms the only effective measure to adopt. Sometimes algae can be removed from above by use of a jet from a fire hose. A grid packing might be cleared by rodding with a long cane but this is laborious and not effective for packings of more than 6-8 feet high.

(v) *Ice Damage*

In winter, icing of packings can produce extensive damage — especially in timber packings. Broken laths or grid trays in successive winters tend to diminish the effective rating of a tower. In such cases broken packing should be replaced and if tower utilisation, position and water temperature is such that icing damage may re-occur in a following season, it is advisable to consult the Cooling Tower Supplier for suggestions for eliminating the trouble.

Distribution System

Periodic inspection of the water distribution system should show at once if there is wrong irrigation. Corrections of troubles are generally simple. The commonest malfunction of a distribution system arises from excessive water being pumped — noticeable when unobstructed distribution pipes and troughs become surcharged and overflow, flooding parts of the packing unevenly. Surging in troughs can often be diminished by use of adjustable wooden baffles. Valves in pipe systems may need slight re-adjustment.

All distribution systems can suffer from sludge or foreign bodies and these can be removed quickly by hand cleaning when fouling is extensive. If distribution employs tubes or weirs, these are more prone to stoppages but can be cleared readily without taking the tower "off the line". Sprays are easily subject to disturbance from foul matter and in some designs can be subject to wear. They should be renewed when they, with their splash cups (if any) show damage, wear or corrosion.

Wooden pipes and troughs in distribution systems require checking. Sometimes a knot shrinks and falls out, leaving a hole to be plugged. Timber joints may open after a tower has been idle for some time — especially in a hot climate — and this may make carpentry repairs desirable. All timber troughs should be checked for level after one year and then every two years.

Not infrequently a water inlet position is carelessly selected by a pipework contractor and distribution is incorrect on account of excess spillage or wrong point of discharge. This is easily seen on inspection.

Shell/Structure

A concrete shell should be regarded as a building and treated likewise. The maintenance requirement is generally insignificant except that some towers merit "Snowcem" or similar external treatment once in five to seven years. When spalling of concrete occurs due to reinforcement corrosion, towers should receive prompt repairs. If the concrete shell is comprised of slabs of pre-cast concrete there is a possibility that vibration (on mechanical draught towers, of course) and admission of water through joints to reinforcement may establish an increased tendency to rusting and spalling, though this does not necessarily follow.

If the shell is of timber this will merely need annual inspection to check damage of coping, handrails, staircase, etc., especially after gales or icing. Spoilation of surface appearance due to leakage following excessive pumping, or storm, or other damage, generally becomes obvious and is easily rectified by a carpenter.

It is particularly important to check that ladders, staircase bracings and handrails remain firm, and that fan casings be kept rigid and of true circular form without touching fan impeller blade tips. If there is risk of the latter occurrence repairs to casings must be prompt and casings reinforced, preferably with steel sections.

Doors need checking that swelling from mist exposure is not excessive.

If structural fixing bolts become weakened from prolonged rusting or corrosion they should be replaced by bronze bolts.

A tower which has been treated with Creosote, when supplied is worth painting with Creosote at intervals of 7/10 years, but a tower treated correctly with copper preservatives should not need further treatment.

Miscellaneous tower components which are often first to need replacement are the mist eliminator (in which fungal decay may be more serious than elsewhere), internal platforms and fan casings and their linings, also air inlet louvres, where fitted.

Where a shell is treated with a skin of ornamental material, e.g. metal sheeting, cement asbestos sheeting, or painted wood panels, maintenance requirements are generally self-evident but sheet steel shells generally require periodic painting outside and, if possible, the inside surfaces should be brushed with a rust inhibitor from time to time. Coloured skins of a shell may merit annual washing from a fire hose.

Pond Basins

Some ponds keep clean and others are prone to algae, leaf or dirt troubles which may lead to obstructions in drains, valves and pumps. If it is possible to evacuate a pond annually for thorough cleaning it is a task which is generally accomplished quickly and permits inspection of penstocks and inlet supply valves and other components not normally readily accessible. It may be necessary in some cases for suction screens to be inspected and cleared at frequent intervals.

Water Treatment Apparatus

From time to time Water Treatment Plant is seen to be neglected. Though installed more from considerations of process plant than for Cooling Tower protection it is worth a reminder that chemical dosage equipment can often suffer severe corrosion and gradually become unreliable if the regular but simple inspection service recommended by makers is neglected.

Glass-fibre cross-flow tower. Air inlet louvres are removable for unrestricted access to pack, fan and shell interior. The laminated glass-fibre casing is completely corrosion proof, needing no painting or maintenance. It is advisable, however, to occasionally wash down coloured casings to maintain their appearance.

chapter 7

WATER TREATMENT

Water Chemistry
Scale
Corrosion
Microbiological Fouling
Silting

---

7. Water Treatment

Some recirculating cooling water installations do not need water treatment. There are, also, installations where, although water treatment is not essential, it should be carefully considered as a means of reducing equipment deterioration and maintenance. In addition, there are other installations where the systems can only be run successfully by the use of carefully selected and operated water treatment.

The ultimate decision concerning any particular system should be the result of discussions between the system designer, operator and water treatment specialist.

Water treatment technology, as most others, has its own set of terms, which could be unfamiliar to some non-specialist engineers. We commence, therefore, with definitions of the more commonly used terms.

TERMINOLOGY OF WATER TREATMENT

Hardness

Salts of calcium and magnesium are quite commonly found dissolved in water supplies. They form insoluble salts when soap is added; and they then separate, forming a surface floating scum. The substances most frequently present in water supplies take the form of bicarbonates, sulphates, chlorides and nitrates of calcium and magnesium. In fresh water, calcium is almost always present in greater quantity than magnesium—not so in the case of sea water, which carries a high concentration of magnesium chloride.

Alkaline Hardness — Temporary Hardness

Calcium and magnesium bicarbonates are both decomposed by the action of heat, part of the carbon dioxide then being released:

$$Ca(HCO_3)_2 \longrightarrow CaCO_3 + H_2O + CO_2$$

Calcium   Calcium
Bicarbonate Carbonate

Since the simple action of heating water will remove bicarbonates, the term "temporary" has been used, although it is now more helpful to use the term "alkaline" hardness as a precise distinction.

Non-Alkaline Hardness — Permanent Hardness

All salts of calcium and magnesium remaining in solution after heating have been termed "permanent" hardness because they do not decompose in the same way when the temperature is raised appreciably. They are now classified as "non-alkaline" hardness.

Alkalinity

The alkaline or "temporary" hardness salts, the bicarbonates, react with mineral acids, releasing carbon dioxide and forming the relevant mineral salts:

$$Ca\,(HCO_3)_2 + H_2SO_4 \longrightarrow CaSO_4 + H_2O + 2CO_2$$

$$\underset{\text{Acid}}{\text{Sulphuric}} \qquad \underset{\text{Sulphate}}{\text{Calcium}}$$

It is because of this reaction with acid that the term "alkaline" hardness is used, with its concomitant "non-alkaline" hardness for the other salts which are neutral and do not react with acid.

Dissolved Solids

The mineral salts found in water can be determined in type and quantity by simple evaporation and weighing residues. In addition to hardness salts — and by other techniques — sodium chloride, sodium sulphate and silica can be found. These substances do not exist in solution as definite compounds, but as "ions" — charged soluble particles of a metal (known as *cations*) or as acid radicles (known as *anions*). The most commonly occurring cations are:

Calcium	Ca^{++}
Magnesium	Mg^{++}
Sodium	Na^+

The most commonly occurring anions are:

Chloride	Cl^{--}
Sulphate	SO_4^{--}
Bicarbonate	HCO_3^{--}

The negative and positive signs indicate polarity of electron charge. The negative signs indicate electron gain, positive signs electron loss. Contaminants can be grouped according to polarity and magnitude of charge.

Suspended Solids

Substances with limited solubility in water are normally removed by filtration. Dust, drawn into a cooling tower as airborne particles can be practically insoluble. It is also necessary to remove by filtration products of corrosion, precipitated temporary hardness, living or dead algae, bacteria and any other precipitates produced by chemical treatment.

Neutrality of Water
pH Value

Pure water dissociates:

$$H_2O \longrightarrow H^+ \quad + \quad OH^-$$

Hydrogen   Hydroxyl
ion   ion

Both hydrogen and hydroxyl ions are present in exactly the same quantity, so that pure water is "neutral". In a unit weight of pure water there will be 0·0000001 unit weights of hydrogen ion and of hydroxyl ion, or 10^{-7} parts of each.

The pH value — the index of acidity, alkalinity or purity — uses the figure 7 as the neutral or purity point on the scale.

Neutral, pure, water, is said to have a pH value of 7.

$pH = \log_{10}(H^+)$. (Where H^+ is the hydrogen ion concentration).

As hydrogen ion concentration is increased the pH value decreases. As hydroxyl ion concentration increases the pH value increases.

Acidity is due to hydrogen ions, so the more acid a water becomes the lower is its pH value; alkalinity is due to hydroxyl ions, so the more alkaline a water becomes the higher is its pH value. This is because acids give hydrogen ions in solution, while alkalis give hydroxyl ions:

$$H_2SO_4 \longrightarrow 2H^+ + SO_4^{--}$$
Sulphuric Acid

$$NaOH \longrightarrow Na^+ + OH^-$$
Caustic Soda

The pH scale covers the range 0-14, from strongly acid to strongly alkaline.

Dissolved Gases

Natural water supplies are usually in equilibrium with the air above them. In cooling towers the water, as fine droplets or thin films in intimate contact with air, attains this equilibrium rapidly. The main gases in air are oxygen and nitrogen; both have limited solubility. Oxygen, which is the gas mostly concerned, has a solubility of about 10 parts per million in water at 10°C.

Other gases may be drawn into cooling water in areas where the atmosphere is polluted. Sulphur dioxide is common in industrial environments and is very soluble; this produces an acid solution. Ammonia, often found in some manufacturing areas, is also very soluble and produces an alkaline solution.

Measurement by Proportion

Both salts and gases, where dissolved or suspended, are usually measured in parts per million — parts by weight. For example: 1,000,000 Kg. of water containing 100 Kg. of sodium chloride or ammonia is said to have a concentration of 100 parts per million (ppm) of sodium chloride or ammonia.

Calcium carbonate is found in all natural water supplies and, as it has a molecular weight of 100, it has become an accepted convention to express all other hardness salts and alkalinity as if they were calcium carbonate.

This simplifies calculation of quantities of water treatment materials. This relationship is sometimes, though not often, applied to sodium chloride and sulphate but never to silica, dissolved gases, suspended solids or, of course, pH value.

Ion Exchange

The terms "water softening" and "base exchange" have become widely known and used. Hardness (i.e. calcium and magnesium) can be removed from water by passing it through a bed of natural resin material known as "Zeolite". In this process, calcium and magnesium salts are exchanged for sodium:

$$CaCl_2 \quad + \quad Na_2Z \longrightarrow CaZ_2 \quad + \quad 2NaCl$$

Calcium	Zeolite	Calcium	Sodium
Chloride		Zeolite	Chloride

The calcium zeolite will only absorb a certian amount of hardness; when capacity is reached the resin bed has to be regenerated using a flushing solution of brine.

$$CaZ_2 \quad + \quad 2NaCl \longrightarrow Na_2Z \quad + \quad CaCl_2$$

Calcium
Chloride

Synthetic resins of high exchange capacity are now used exclusively.

It is possible to remove alkaline hardness selectively by choice of a special resin in its hydrogen form, i.e. one that has been regenerated with acid instead of brine:

$$Ca(HCO_3)_2 \quad + \quad H_2Z \longrightarrow CaZ \quad + \quad 2H_2CO_3$$

Carbonic
Acid

The carbonic acid can be further decomposed by air scrubbing:

$$H_2CO_3 \longrightarrow H_2O \quad + \quad CO_2$$

Carbon
Dioxide

This produces a water which will not form scale since it has a lower proportion of dissolved salts due to the alkaline hardness originally present in the water being removed.

The other type of ion exchange plant which may be met with is "deionisation" or "demineralisation".

All cations, or metals, are removed by one resin:

$$H_2C \quad + \quad 2NaCl \longrightarrow 2HCl \quad + \quad Na_2C$$

Cation
Resin

The anions, or acid radicles are removed by another resin:

$$AOH \quad + \quad HCl \longrightarrow HOH \quad + \quad ACl$$

Anion	Water from
Resin	these two operations.

 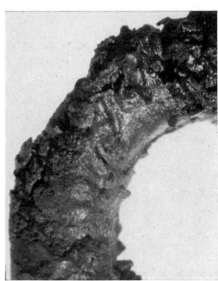

Left: Section of 'U' carbon steel tube approximately 1″ overall diameter before exposure to untreated cooling water. Right: the same tube after test run. The cooling water involved had high chloride and high hardness content.

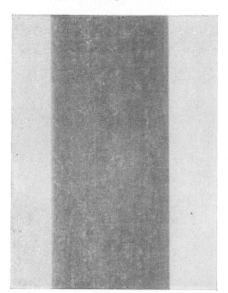 

As above – showing straight section of test tubing.

The only product is water. Very pure water free from all mineral salts is produced by this process. Resins are regenerated by acid and caustic soda.

Fully demineralised water is not economical for the normal cooling tower system.

PROBLEMS CAUSED BY WATER

It should be realised that it is not water itself which causes problems in cooling tower systems, but the impurities dissolved in it, or carried by it. These problems fall into four categories.

1. Scale

2. Corrosion

3. Microbiological Fouling

4. Silting.

Each of these is dealt with in turn — showing how it occurs and how it can be prevented.

Scale

Calcium and magnesium bicarbonates are decomposed by heat to form their respective carbonates — and by the scrubbing action of the cooling water spray which removes some carbon dioxide. Heat exchange surfaces, where water is used as a heat absorber, are particularly prone to deposits of calcium carbonate. Magnesium carbonate is fairly soluble, but will decompose further to insoluble magnesium hydroxide:

$$MgCO_3 + H_2O \longrightarrow Mg(OH)_2 + CO_2$$

Polyphosphates are sometimes added to cooling water as corrosion inhibitors: these are converted — by heat, high or low pH values, and also long-term retention in the system — to orthophosphates which form insoluble calcium and magnesium salts. Such salts will inevitably be deposited as scale.

Calcium sulphate (calcium and sulphate ions are invariably present in water), is not a very soluble salt, and its solubility decreases as the temperature increases.

Concentration of mineral salts

Where operational water temperature does not exceed more than 140°F it is sound practice to purge a proportion of the cooling system water when the product of calcium ion and sulphate ion concentrations exceeds 500,000. This figure must include any sulphate introduced by acid dosing. This is explained below.

Scale problems in a cooling system are mainly due to this concentration of mineral salts, those which are normally soluble are increased to the limit of their solubility as evaporation proceeds; bicarbonates are the least soluble of all salts found in natural water supplies. Thermal decomposition adds to scale deposits.

Acid Dosing

If bicarbonate could be converted into the more soluble form the problem is at once solved by keeping these salts permanently in solution. This is readily done by acid dosing — sulphuric acid being most commonly used — since it is cheaper than any other. By adding enough acid to keep the alkalinity of the cooling water below 100 ppm (except where metal temperatures are higher than normal) and a pH value below 7 can be maintained, it is possible to avoid deposits of calcium carbonate.

Acid dosing, or simple alkaline reduction, is the most reliable method for preventing scale and is the most widely used.

Base Exchange

Removal of hardness by the base exchange process will, of course, completely prevent scale. This is a process often used but is not the best overall approach. In most cases it is only alkaline hardness which causes scale but since the base exchange softening process also removes non-alkaline hardness — unnecessarily — both the size of plant and the cost of regeneration are larger than need be.

This method of softening produces sodium bicarbonate which, since it is alkaline, leads to a high pH value for the circulating water — well over 8·0. Values of alkalinity of this order are the cause of lignin being leached out of cooling tower timbers (delignification). This is accelerated where chlorine is present.

Starvation or Dealkalisation

A much better process uses the "starvation" or "dealkalisation" method described earlier, for removal of alkaline hardness alone. This is, in fact, an alternative means of acid dosing — external to the cooling system.

With this method, purge is greatly reduced, because of the reduction in dissolved salts.

Because there is a considerably lower water requirement the capital cost of a "starvation" plant can be justified, particularly for large cooling systems. Compared with base exchange, regeneration costs are considerably lower.

The Langelier Index

For many years the "Langelier Index" was used, and was very popular in assisting simultaneous control of scale and corrosion.

Analysis of the cooling water compared with the Index showed whether scale would form or corrosion would take place. If corrosion were indicated the pH value of the water was adjusted towards neutral. If scale formation were indicated a small quantity of polyphosphate (or a mixture of tannin with polyphosphate) would be added as a stabiliser.

This particular approach had one major disadvantage: it is dependent on temperature. As the temperature varies the water can be either scale forming or corrosive, thus contradicting the indication of the Index. The

Index method is quite unreliable in fluctuating conditions and has now been largely superseded by the more reliable methods described.

Automatic pH control

For maximum operational efficiency the addition of acid to a cooling water system should be controlled by an automatic pH detector. An electrode and relay system is used to start and stop acid dosage either by pump or pneumatic valve.

Careful separation of electrode and dosing points are essential; the specialist equipment manufacturers normally advise in individual cases.

Calculation of Purge Rate

Cooling water salts concentrated by evaporation result in deposits of low solubility. Although calcium carbonate deposits can be prevented by the use of acid, care has to be taken to avoid reaching the solubility limit of calcium sulphate (and calcium phosphate where phosphates are used in the water treatment programme).

In the absence of deliberate purging, drift loss and/or windage from a cooling tower determines the concentration. The maximum concentration which would be attained is calculated from the following equation:

$$Z \text{ max} = \frac{V + D}{D}$$

Where Z max = maximum concentration
V   = loss due to evaporation
D   = loss due to drift and/or windage

Evaporation loss is approximately one per cent of the circulation rate for every 10°F fall in temperature across the tower. The drift and windage losses will be a total of approximately 0·2% of the circulation rate for a mechanical draught tower and about 0·5% for a natural draught tower.

For example, for a mechanical draught tower with a temperature drop of 20°F the maximum concentration possible would be:

$$\frac{2 + 0·2}{0·2} \text{ or } 11 \text{ times}$$

Once this figure has been determined a decision has to be made — whether this maximum can be allowed or whether it has to be reduced. Tables of solubility data for calcium sulphate or phosphate are normally consulted as a guide and permissible system concentration Z lim, established. Then:

$$\text{Purge Rate} = \frac{V}{Z_{lim} - 1} - D$$

If phosphate inhibition is intended a maximum concentration of five might be permitted for an installation. With an evaporation of 100 gpm and windage loss of 10 gpm

$$\text{Purge Rate} = \frac{100}{4} - 10 = 15 \text{ gpm}$$

Chloride concentration is usually used as the control measure. All chlorides in cooling water are very soluble and concentrate at a known steady rate.

Purge may also be controlled by means of a conductivity detector, which activates the opening of a purge valve at a pre-determined maximum value.

Corrosion

Ferrous metals in cooling systems are those most likely to corrode, and, once this process has begun, it will continue at a rapid rate. Corrosion, an electrochemical phenomenon, follows establishment of cells, complete with anodes and cathodes, cooling water acting as the essential electrolyte.

Electrolytic corrosion cells result from many different causes, e.g., metal alloying, metal differences, scale, organic fouling (encouraged or added to by contamination from industrial processes) the products of corrosion itself and variations in dissolved oxygen resulting from thermal changes. Basically, cell reaction changes can be expressed as follows:

1. Anodically: $Fe \longrightarrow Fe^{++} + 2e$
   Iron is dissolved.

2. Cathodically: $O + 2e + H_2O \longrightarrow 2OH^-$
   An hydroxyl ion is produced which reacts with the iron in solution to form the corrosion product, ferrous hydroxide.

$$Fe^{++} + 2OH^- \longrightarrow Fe(OH)_2$$

Local Inhibitors

When these reactions were first understood, attempts were made to control this corrosion by adding material which would block either the anode or the cathode, thus acting as local inhibitors.

Chromatics, nitrites and alkaline metal hydroxides form anodic inhibitors, whilst bicarbonates and zinc derivatives act cathodically. Polyphosphates, while primarily cathodic, will usually produce a proportion of anodic inhibiting orthophosphates.

Prevention of these reactions depends upon the production of a continuous film or deposit which, anodically, may be iron oxide or a mixture of iron oxide and chromic oxide; cathodically, either calcium carbonate, zinc hydroxide or zinc phosphate.

All of these methods have been used extensively, but they all have the disadvantage that they need comparatively large quantities for acceptable inhibiting action. This is particularly so where a high chloride or sulphate content is present. Sodium chromate and sodium nitrite, for example, must be held between 300 and 1,000 ppm depending upon the corrosion potential of the water.

Alkalinity

For the reasons given, corrosion can be slightly reduced by making water alkaline, but since this may precipitate calcium salts, which are only slightly soluble at increased pH levels, and alkalinity can also lead to loss of lignin in cooling tower timbers, it is not the complete answer.

Cooling water side of tube bundle in an air compressor heat exchanger showing fouling by organic slimes.

In soft water areas, where structural and other materials are not likely to be harmed, some inhibiting effect can be obtained — but much more effective methods are available and desirable.

Simultaneous anodic and cathodic inhibitors

Where cooling water can be treated with an inhibitor which operates simultaneously anodically and cathodically corrosion will be effectively prevented.

This highly specialised technique is now widely used. It is most effective and is capable of reducing corrosion to very low levels. This combination technique has the added advantage of requiring much less material for a greatly increased inhibitor action than any attempt to exert control separately over anodic or cathodic corrosion.

The production of compounds for this dual purpose employs zinc salts as cathodic inhibitors blended with chromates, organic passivators or polyphosphates. In addition there may be complex organic compounds which, by acting as overall absorption inhibitors supplement the overall function.

Fortunately, measurement of the rate at which corrosion occurs is simple. The efficacy of compound inhibitors has been fully proved by many extensive and individually measured trials. In circumstances where uninhibited corrosion was proceeding at the rate of 50/150 mils. (0·05-0·15 in.) per year, the rate was reduced to below 5 mils. per year (0·005 in.).

This method of measurement is standardised for carbon steel and process operating temperatures of 300/350°C.

The inhibitor concentrations involved were between 40 and 100 ppm. Treatment of this type gives excellent protection and is very economical.

Microbiological Fouling

Cooling system make-up water very often contains live micro-organisms. Industrial intakes frequently can be contaminated with sewage waste and once the cooling water system is open to the atmosphere at any point airborne organisms will start to circulate.

Water used for cooling purposes will often have pockets or areas in the system where, unavoidably, temperatures will be ideal for encouraging rapid growth of any of these living materials. Spray oxygenation and the unavoidable and accidental inclusion of such nutrients as phosphates, hydrocarbons and ammonia encourage proliferation.

The variety of such organisms is very wide. They can be classified broadly as: algae, bacteria (aerobic and anaerobic), fungi and moulds.

Algae are identifiable by colour — green or blue-green; they thrive only in daylight, being dependent on photosynthesis. Although algae are found mostly in exposed areas of the cooling tower and open ponds, dead material floats away and is circulated round the system. Very little of this debris is needed to block tubes, tube plates and circulating mains. Algae aid in production of scale by absorbing carbon dioxide from the water, thus promoting breakdown of soluble bicarbonates to yield the insoluble carbonates which deposit as scale. In the process of liberating oxygen, corrosion is stimulated.

Bacteria, unlike algae, develop rapidly out of the light and when totally enclosed. If not checked, bacteria will block the system, with or without help from algae, in just the same way.

Both algae and bacteria produce slimes which encourage electrolytic corrosion cells by preventing inhibitors from forming protective films on metal surfaces. Slime-laden cooling systems are particularly prone to pitting corrosion.

Anaerobic bacteria, particularly those known as "sulphate reducers" or iron bacteria, are present, but dormant, in all natural water supplies, ready to proliferate on encountering favourable temperatures and/or nutrients.

Sulphates in cooling water supplies are reduced by anaerobic bacteria to hydrogen sulphide, rapidly attacking steel, and producing deeply pitting corrosion.

Fungi can produce the same effect, though it is less usual for them to do so.

These groups of living organisms can be easily suppressed by the use of chlorine gas, a material which is widely available, supplied in cylinders ready for use. Relatively simple equipment is used for dosing, either continuously, or at pre-set intervals.

Since virtually all water supplies used for cooling purposes have some organic and/or ammonia content, a part of any chlorine used will be lost by immediate reaction and since a surplus of "free" chlorine is essential for biocidal purposes the initial demand must be catered for. This may easily exceed by several parts per million the dosage required.

Maintenance of a free chlorine content of 0·5-1·0 ppm measured at the water inlet to the cooling tower is essential. The required rate of chlorine addition is determined by measuring the difference in chlorine concentration between water entering and leaving the cooling tower. The major loss is by aeration and absorption by timber. Excessive chlorination must be avoided — to prevent timber degradation and loss of structural strength. If the water circulating in the tower is too highly alkaline (pH exceeding 8) the timber degradation will be accelerated due to the solubility of lignin in alkali.

Sodium Hypochlorite

The practical use of chlorine gas is restricted to comparatively large industrial cooling systems on account of the cost of dosage equipment. As an alternative, sodium hypochlorite, essentially in alkaline chlorine solution, is used to provide a source of chlorine not requiring special methods of application.

Non-oxidising Biocides

Smaller cooling systems, including those used for air conditioning, use organic materials toxic to living organisms.

Unlike chlorine, which is an oxidising agent, these materials are known as non-oxidising biocides.

These materials have no adverse effect on structural timbers or other materials and are equally effective at top and bottom of the tower as well as in the open pond.

The most widely used basic materials are chlorinated phenols, alternatively the organo-tin compounds, quarternary ammonium salts and selective mono- and diamines.

Broad Spectrum Biocides

Specific groups of organisms react differently and require individual treatment. Where a system is badly polluted with many different types of organisms a mixed biocide is used with broad spectrum coverage.

Shock Dosage

Normally, application requires the addition of the liquid treatment as a shock dose applied to the water in the tower pond.

Frequency of dosage is usually dependent upon skilled observations of biological activity, or, more precisely, by laboratory use of microbiological examination and colony counting techniques.

It is most often found that intervals of three to seven days between shock dosages suffice to maintain control. Exceptions occur when unusual quantities of nutrient materials find their way into the circulating water. Unusual ambient or process temperature conditions may produce a similar effect. These conditions can occur suddenly but, once detected, can be overcome by increasing the frequency and/or strength of shock dosage.

Fouling Deposits

Strictly, fouling refers to any type of deposit which forms on metal surfaces in cooling systems. It has already been shown how it is possible to deal with deposits of hardness salts, corrosion products and micro-biological growth. An additional cause arises from the mixture of silt and mud drawn into cooling water by the scrubbing action of water and spray and, sometimes, from make-up water taken directly from a stream or canal.

These insoluble solids build up by concentration in the same way as do soluble salts and are more difficult to control.

Until recent years, the only methods of removal that were used or considered possible, were physical cleaning or the use of acid. These methods had to be used at fairly frequent intervals to maintain even reasonable plant efficiency. In addition, both methods required the plant to be shut down.

Chemical Additives

Chemical additives are now available which perform the function of antifoulants. They are classified, according to mode of action, as chelants or sequestrants, dispersants or coagulants. These materials are capable of preventing suspended insoluble solids from becoming immovable solid deposits in water cooled equipment.

Those deposits containing a majority of calcium, magnesium, iron and aluminium salts can be kept in solution in the form of stable complexes by means of chelants or sequestrants. Molecular bonding of the metal irons keeps the affected material in solution.

Absorption is the key to the function of dispersants and coagulants. Molecules of the additive material absorb the particles of foreign matter. By preventing agglomeration of particle size the total amount of contaminating material can be kept dispersed throughout the total volume of water available.

Coagulants work in entirely the opposite way, but by producing a completely controlled mass of material, density can be reduced. A loose, fluffy floc results, which, having a density close to that of water, cannot form a hard deposit.

Any, or all, of the special properties of these materials may be used, singly or in combination, depending upon the type of fouling that must be controlled.

Dosing is either continuous or intermittent, preferably the former.

It is now the practice for corrosion inhibitors to have anti-fouling materials compounded with them. Multi-purpose water treatments are now perfectly practicable and are coming rapidly into everyday use.

Mechanical Filtration

Suspended solids which produce insoluble fouling products can be prevented from entering the system by mechanical filtration, which need only be brought into operation on those occasions when local climatic or other conditions produce heavy pollution.

This type of filtration cannot deal with air-borne contamination introduced by open-type cooling towers — a severe problem in some industrial areas.

Mechanical filtration still has to be employed in such circumstances. Side-stream methods are used: a proportion of the circulating water passes through either pressure-type sand-bed filters or cartridges that can be cleaned or renewed. The proportion of the total volume of circulating water cleaned in this way controls the total time for which the plant is kept in action.

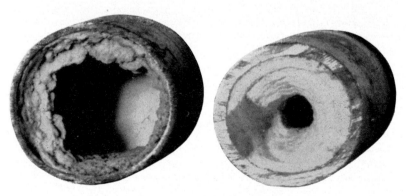

Scale formation in pipes

chapter 8

INDUSTRIAL APPLICATIONS

8. Industrial Applications

Evaporative water cooling towers are used for a very large number of applications.

However, nearly all these applications fall into the following major categories:—

(a) Refrigeration Plant.

(b) Compressor Cooling.

(c) Engine Cooling.

(d) Metallurgical Processes.

(e) Plastic Moulding Machine Cooling.

(f) Chemical and Refinery Plant Cooling.

(g) Turbine Condenser Cooling.

Each of these requires its own special treatment. There are different temperature levels, methods of control, and pipe layouts.

The different methods necessary are described below:—

(a) REFRIGERATION PLANT

In refrigeration processes, the heat absorbed evaporates the refrigerant. The refrigerant is then compressed, condensed and passed once again to the evaporator via an expansion valve.

In the condenser, the most common coolant, used to absorb the latent heat of condensation of the refrigerant, is water.

Condensing Temperature

The majority of water-cooled refrigeration condensers have a condensing temperature between 95°F and 115°F. The lower the condensing temperature the lower will be the power input to the compressor for a given refrigeration load. Unfortunately, lower condensing temperatures require low water temperatures, resulting in larger cooling towers. Judgment is required to strike an economic balance.

Generally speaking, for each ton of refrigeration (12,000 Btu/hr.), the amount of heat to be removed from the condenser is about 14,400 Btu/hr. This could be accomplished by circulating 144 gallons of water per hour, with a temperature difference of 10°F across the condenser.

A good compromise between condenser and tower size, and compressor power is obtained with water temperatures of about 90°F on and 80°F off the cooling tower.

These figures relate, of course, to common design temperatures in U.K. plants. Appreciably higher temperatures are normally acceptable for plants in hotter climates but even when high air wet bulb temperatures prevail, cooling tower approach temperatures are seldom onerous.

Factors Affecting Condensing Temperature

For a given refrigeration plant its performance will depend on a number of factors. Two of these concern the engineer who is designing the cooling tower. These are (a) Water temperatures, (b) Overall heat transfer co-efficient in the condenser.

Increased water temperatures result in increased condensing temperature, with a consequently reduced refrigeration capacity and possibly an over-loaded compressor motor.

Water temperatures may rise because the ambient air wet bulb temperature is higher than that on which the tower was designed. Increased water temperatures can also result when the flow of water is restricted by dirt deposition or scale formation on the condenser tubes. It is usual to fit gauges to record pressure drop across the condenser to detect this and many condensers have removable ends to facilitate tube cleaning. The deposition of solids on the tubes affects the heat transfer coefficient, even when flow is only slightly reduced. Again the effect is to increase condensing temperature.

Control of Condensing Temperature

Constant condensing temperatures are essential for correct operation of the refrigeration plant. As the temperature of the water from the tower varies with air wet bulb temperature and load variation, some form of control is necessary. There are two main methods which are:—

(i) *Direct Control*

With this system the refrigerant pressure (which is directly related to the condensing temperature) is used to control the water flow to the condenser by means of a valve.

The small by-pass ensures that water always flows through the pump to prevent overheating (Fig. 30).

(ii) *Indirect*

A temperature sensing element on the condenser flow line operates a three-way mixing valve on the pump suction. This ensures a constant flow of water at a controlled temperature.

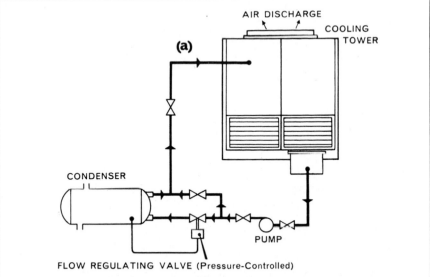

Fig. 30. **Cooling circuit schematic for direct control of condenser head pressure.**

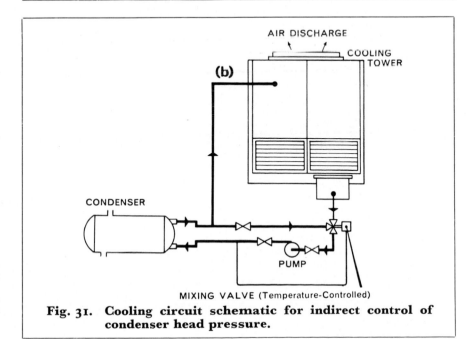

Fig. 31. **Cooling circuit schematic for indirect control of condenser head pressure.**

The system is said to be indirect because it controls water temperature, not condensing temperature. The system is not desirable if an unloading compressor (with consequently wide variation in load) is used. (In an absorption refrigeration system, however, this method of control is normal practice) (Fig. 31).

Installation

The diagram shows the basic water connections and accessories.

Flexible connections are required on the condenser pipework when the refrigeration unit is on anti-vibration mountings. Isolating valves enable the condenser to be taken out of circuit for cleaning when the tubes become scaled.

Water treatment apparatus is essential if frequent de-scaling is to be avoided, where water has a high content of solids.

It is advisable to provide electrical interlocks to controllers of circulation pump and compressor pump motors to shut down the refrigeration plant, in the event of failure of either of these motors.

Medium/Large Tonnage Plant

Where there is a wide Summer/Winter or Night/Day variation of re-frigeration duty on substantial plants, good refrigeration design practice generally incorporates flexible control of two or more compressors. The condensers of these plants may be served economically by a cooling tower with several cells, each of which can be manually or automatically put into or out of action as refrigeration load changes. Alternatively, a cooling tower may have its cell or cells fed by variable quantity of air, through the medium of two-speed or multi-speed fan motors, or variable pitch impellers.

(b) AIR COMPRESSORS

Compressed air is playing an ever-increasing part in production engineering and therefore the air compressor is an increasingly common piece of equipment.

When air is compressed, its temperature rises, heating the cylinder walls. It is necessary to cool these to prevent material failure. Small machines can be air cooled, but most compressors have water-cooled jackets.

When the compression takes place in stages, intercoolers are usually incorporated and many compressors are also fitted with aftercoolers. In both cases, these are used to reduce the temperature of the compressed air, and are usually water cooled.

The amount of water required will vary with the make of compressor and the quantity of air being handled. Table 7, reproduced from the Handbook of the B.C.A.S., gives the water requirements in terms of suction air volume.

TABLE 7

Water flow in gpm per 100 cfm F.A.D.

Equipment to be cooled	Water Inlet Temperatures in °F			
	60	70	80	90
Aftercooler or intercooler separate (80/100 p.s.i.g. 2-stage compression)	2.5	3.0	3.5	4.0
Intercooler and jacket in series (80/100 p.s.i.g. 2-stage compression)	2.9	3.4	3.8	4.5
Aftercooler (80/100 p.s.i.g. 1-stage compression)	4.0	4.5	5.2	6.0
Both high and low pressure jackets with water separate from intercooler (80/100 p.s.i.g. 2-stage compression)	1.0	1.1	1.2	1.4
Jacket (40 p.s.i.g. 1-stage compression)	0.6	0.7	0.8	0.9
Jacket (60 p.s.i.g. 1-stage compression)	0.9	1.0	1.1	1.2
Jacket (80 p.s.i.g. 1-stage compression)	1.2	1.3	1.4	1.5
Jacket (100 p.s.i.g. 1-stage compression)	1.5	1.6	1.7	1.8

e.g. 250 c.f.m. single stage machine 100 p.s.i.g. with aftercooler, assuming 75°F water temperature, requires:

Aftercooler 2.5 × 4.85 × 60 — 727.5 g.p.h.
Jacket   2.5 × 1.65 × 60 = 247.5 g.p.h.   Total = 975.0 g.p.h.

Water temperature rise, based on the above flow rates, will be about 15-20°F. There are a number of factors governing this, of course, and the manufacturer will give the correct value for each installation.

The pipework layout is quite simple, as shown in Fig. 32 (a) and (b).

Controls

It is usual, for reasons of economy, to wire the coils of the cooling tower pump and fan starters in series with the compressor motor starter coil. This ensures the tower working only when the compressor is in use.

In the event of pump failure, a pressure switch in the delivery line can prevent damage to the machine by shutting down the compressor motor.

Further economy can be obtained by controlling the tower fan by a thermostat, either in the tower tank or in the water return pipe to the compressor. This will shut off the fan when the water temperature falls below the design figure, as it will when the ambient air wet bulb temperature is low.

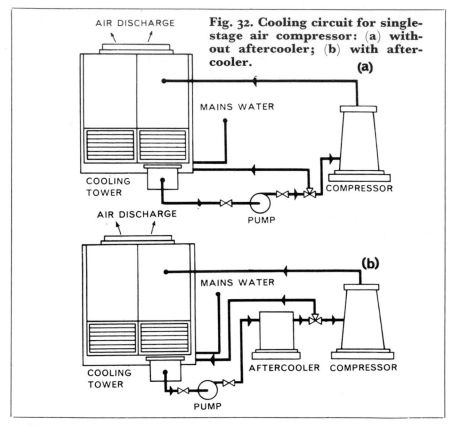

AIR DISCHARGE

Fig. 32. Cooling circuit for single-stage air compressor: (a) without aftercooler; (b) with aftercooler.

(a)

MAINS WATER

COOLING TOWER

COMPRESSOR

AIR DISCHARGE

PUMP

(b)

MAINS WATER

COOLING TOWER

AFTERCOOLER COMPRESSOR

PUMP

General

Cooling water quantities for air compressors are invariably much smaller than are required for most refrigeration plants hence their cooling towers are smaller. It is not uncommon to find small water coolers for compressor cooling located inside factories, a practice to be deprecated unless air is ducted to the inlet of the cooling tower from outside the building to ensure the lowest air wet bulb temperatures for cooling.

(c) ENGINES

In many respects, engine cooling is similar to compressor cooling (Fig. 33). Heat from the combustion process must be removed from the cylinders, as well as associated ancillary equipment such as oil coolers and intercoolers.

Generally, water temperatures are higher than with a compressor, since in this case high cylinder wall temperatures (if controlled) are desirable.

Water temperatures in the order of 160°F to 180°F are often encountered. Typical heat dissipation rates, flow rates and temperatures are given in Table 8.

TABLE 8

Equipment	Heat Dissipation Rate Btu./hr./h.p.	Water Temperatures On	Off	Water Flow Rate Gal./hr./h.p.
Jacket Water	1,500 — 2,000	110°F	130°F	8—12
Oil Cooler	250 — 300	105°F	110°F	6—12
Intercooler	250 — 300	80°F	90°F	4—12

This table is only to give a guide to values encountered in practice. The actual rates and temperatures will vary with the type of engine, manufacturer, speed, horsepower and even site conditions.

A very simple arrangement is obtained when the jacket and oil cooler circuits (and even the charge cooler) are connected in series (Fig. 34).

Frequently, a smaller quantity of water is required for the charge cooler than the oil cooler or jacket; in these cases a by-pass line is used and the diagrammatic arrangement is as shown in Fig. 35.

Effect of Changing Water Temperature

It is most important that the design water temperatures are maintained. In the case of the jacket and oil cooling circuits, manufacturers often specify maximum and *minimum* temperatures, advising thermostatic control.

Variation in the water temperature to the intercooler on charge-cooled engines will affect the power output of the engines. Such engines are usually rated according to BSS. 649:1958 which lays down a standard temperature of 75°F. Where this is exceeded the engine power will be reduced.

For every increase of 10°F the reduction or "de-rating" will be between 3% and 5% of full load.

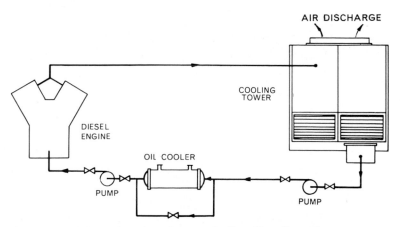

Fig. 33. Cooling circuit schematic for diesel engine.

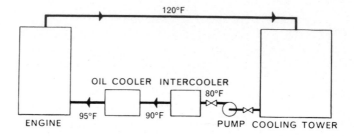

Fig. 34. Typical water temperature in a diesel engine cooling circuit which includes an intercooler and an oil cooler.

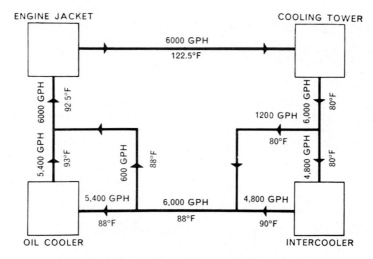

Fig. 35. Typical water flow rates and temperatures in a diesel engine cooling circuit including intercooler and oil cooler by-pass circuits.

In this country 75°F is a temperature well within the capabilities of the evaporative cooling tower. Overseas, in the Middle East for example, where air wet bulb temperatures of 80°F or more occur, engine sizes must be increased for a given output.

This de-rating sometimes makes it necessary for the two cooling circuits to be separated. One cooling tower is used for the jacket and oil coolers, with a separate cooling tower operating at lower water temperatures for the intercooler.

Using a small tower for the intercooler, cooling to about 75°F and a separate tower for the jacket and oil coolers, operated at higher temperatures, can be more economic than one tower which would have to cool the total water circulation to 75°F. However, the large quantities requiring cooling are always for jacket cooling water. Therefore the modern tendency seems to be the maintenance of such high re-cooled water temperatures that natural draught towers or atmospheric cooling frames are often sufficient for this duty.

(d) METALLURGICAL PROCESSES

1. Bright Annealing Furnaces

The most common application of cooling water in this field is in Continuous Bright Annealing Furnaces. In this type of furnace the metal being treated is moved through the furnace by various methods such as mattress conveyors or rollers. A typical furnace of this type is shown in Fig. 36.

There are tunnels leading to and from the heating zone, which is usually maintained at about 850°C for steel and 550°C for brass and similar non-ferrous alloys.

The whole of the interior of the furnace and tunnels is filled with a protective atmosphere to prevent scaling. Also, it is necessary for the metal leaving the end of the cooling tunnel to be below about 250°C to prevent oxidation. To achieve this the tunnel is cooled by water flowing through jackets in the top and bottom.

Fig. 36. Cooling Tunnel on Wellman-Incandescent Bright Annealing Furnace.

Manufacturers usually stipulate that cooling water is required at 75°-80°F. The heat that will be picked up by the cooling water is calculated as follows:

It is a safe assumption that all heat given up by the metal in cooling in the exit tunnel will enter the water. In addition, any heat given up by the hot gas leaving the hot zone and passing down the tunnels will also enter the cooling water.

Thus the heat given up to the cooling water in the cooling tunnel by the metal will be the product of the rate of flow of metal, the specific heat of the metal, and the temperature drop of the metal between the hot zone and the exit of the cooling tunnel. If the metal parts are supported on trays, then the heat carried down the tunnel by these must also be allowed for in a similar way. (The heat given up by the protective atmosphere in flowing down the tunnel can be calculated by the same method. For safety, assume that the gas leaves the tunnel at the same temperature as the metal).

The permitted temperature rise of the cooling water is usually stipulated by the furnace manufacturer and will be about 10°-15°F. Thus from the cooling load calculated in Btu./hr. and the temperature rise in °F the required water flow rate can be found.

The protective atmosphere generators used with these furnaces also require cooling. The cooling water flow rate and temperatures required must be obtained from the manufacturer. Normally, the cooling water temperature on to the gas generator is about 75°-80°F, with a temperature rise of about 30°F. The flow rates required can vary from a few g.p.m. up to as much as 50 g.p.m. depending upon the size of plant.

In another type of annealing furnace, the metal being annealed is placed in a sealed container or 'pot', which is filled with a protective atmosphere. This pot is then heated, in the furnace, to the annealing temperature.

After removal from the furnace the pot is left to cool by radiating heat to the atmosphere for a period up to an hour, after which, water is allowed to pour over it, providing further cooling.

The period of water cooling is quite long and may last anything from 10-15 hours while the pot temperature falls to about 50°C. During this period the gas inside the pot is also cooled by water circulation in a closed circuit to prevent a high temperature gradient.

The total amount of heat rejected is found, as before, from the product of weight of metal being annealed, specific heat, and temperature difference. The rate at which heat is dissipated is, however, widely variable and therefore, initially the water temperature will be at or near boiling point and finally will approach the pot temperature of 50°C.

The heat dissipation curve is shown below (Fig. 37).

To smooth out these temperature fluctuations a balance tank is incorporated in the circuit. This contains a large quantity of water compared to the amount in circulation, and therefore the resulting variations in temperature are small. The circuit is shown below.

Two pumps are necessary, as there are now two breaks in the water circuit (Fig. 38).

The pot is usually cooled in a closed compartment or spray chamber to prevent the loss of water in the form of steam.

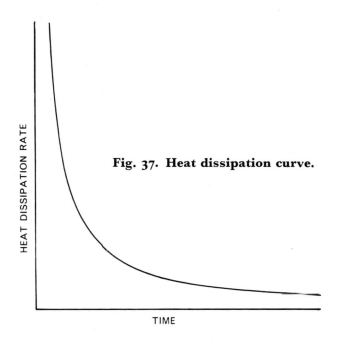

Fig. 37. Heat dissipation curve.

TIME

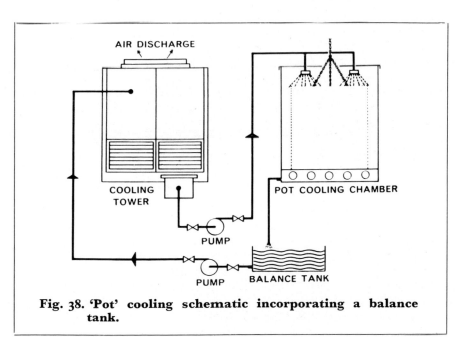

Fig. 38. 'Pot' cooling schematic incorporating a balance tank.

2. Induction Furnaces

Other furnaces, used for melting or ingot heating, require cooling to protect the materials of construction from the high temperatures involved.

A common type is the induction furnace, where high energy electrical currents are induced in the metal load, thereby inducing heat from within.

In these cases cooling coils are built into the furnace walls and water is circulated to prevent excessive temperatures. On the outlet side, the coils are arranged to discharge into an open tundish or tank to provide visual proof that water is flowing.

Again, there are two points where the circuit is broken and consequently two pumps must be provided. A typical arrangement is shown in Fig. 39 below.

Because of the importance of maintaining water flow at all times when the furnace is in use, precautions are taken to prevent accidental damage.

The two pumps are electrically interlocked to prevent one tank being drained and the other overfilled. As it is difficult to precisely balance the pumps, a float switch is used to control the level of the small collecting tank. In this case the interlock is one-way and pump 'A' is started only by the float switch.

A pressure switch on the discharge of pump 'B' prevents the furnace being switched on without water flowing. A time switch is often incorporated to ensure that the cooling water continues to flow after the furnace is switched off. This removes the residual heat from the furnace walls.

3. Quenching

Quenching is the rapid cooling of hot metals by plunging them into a tank of water or oil. The metal is often at about 1,000°C before entering the quench. Consequently, a large amount of heat enters the liquid in the quench tank in a very short time, one minute being a typical quench time.

Where there is insufficient time between quenches to permit the temperature of the quench liquid to return to normal, it is necessary to remove

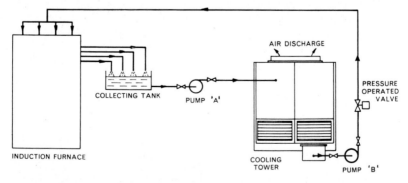

Fig. 39 Schematic of cooling circuit for an induction furnace.

heat continuously from the tank. How this is done depends on whether the quenching medium is water or oil.

(i) *Water*

In this case water from the tank can be pumped direct to the cooling tower before being returned by gravity (Fig. 40).

(ii) *Oil*

In this case it is necessary to circulate the oil through a water cooled heat exchanger and back to the tank. The cooling water is circulated through the heat exchanger and the cooling tower. The system is shown in Fig. 41.

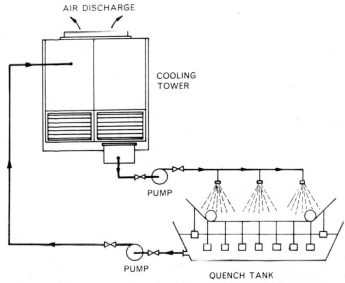

Fig. 40. Schematic of cooling circuit for a continuous quench tank using water sprays.

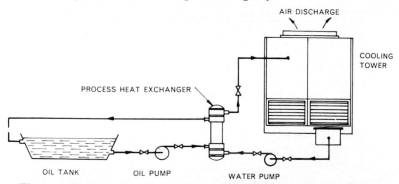

Fig. 41. Schematic of cooling circuit for an oil quench using an oil/water heat exchanger.

In both cases the cooling load on the cooling tower can be taken as equal to the rate at which heat is rejected to the tank by the metal being quenched. This is the product of the lb/h. of metal, the temperature through which it is being cooled and the specific heat of the metal.

The desirable temperature of the metal being quenched, and of the quench liquid, is determined by the metallurgist. However, the circulation rates of water and oil are chosen by the engineer designing the cooling system, and should be selected to give the most economical cooling tower or combination of cooling tower and heat exchanger, as the case may be.

It should be mentioned that some quench plants function at rather long intervals when automatic or remote control of the cooling tower fan may be justified.

4. Degreasing

Degreasing tanks are used for removing oily depositions from metal. One type consists of a tank, at the bottom of which is a liquid organic solvent — usually trichlorethylene. Heaters drive off vapour which rises up and surrounds the metal being degreased. Trichlorethylene vapour is toxic and therefore, for reasons of safety as well as economy, has to be prevented from spilling out of the tank (it is heavier than air). This is achieved by a cooling coil placed near the top of the tank, as shown in Fig. 42. Cooling water is passed through the coil condensing the vapour which falls to the bottom of the tank.

Mains water can be used for cooling but many Water Authorities enforce regulations which make it an offence to connect directly to the mains. Therefore, the use of a mains water break tank with ball valve and a circulating pump are required. By substituting a cooling tower for this tank, the cost of cooling can be considerably reduced.

A typical cooling system comprising cooling coil, pump, pipework and cooling tower is shown in Fig. 43.

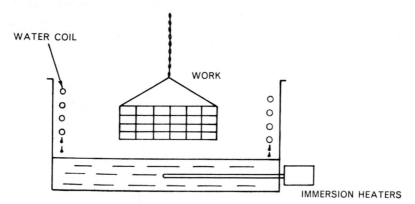

Fig. 42. Schematic showing principle of operation of a degreasing tank.

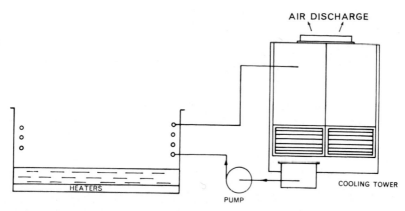

Fig. 43. Schematic of cooling circuit for a degreasing tank.

The heater at the bottom of the tank is often electrical. In such a case it would be prudent to electrically interlock the electric heater with the cooling tower fan and pump. This would ensure that the immersion heater could not be switched into circuit unless the cooling system was fully operative.

The calculation of cooling duty for the tower is a simple matter. It may be assumed that the rate that heat enters the cooling water is equal to the output from the heater. The water temperature entering the cooling coil should be about 75°-80°F, and the temperature rise of the water about 30°F: Given these three facts the flow rate can be found quite easily.

The cooling coil is particularly susceptible to blockage by scale deposition, particularly if the make-up water to the cooling tower is hard, therefore water treatment and blowdown are often necessary.

(e) PLASTIC MOULDING MACHINES

These machines are simple examples of single circuit cooling duty, with small water flows even for large machines. But, as the plastics industry expands, more production shops are established with numbers of moulding machines for which the aggregate cooling water demand is substantial and for which a tower may pay for itself in 12-24 months.

Unfortunately, few injection moulding machine makers seem to determine heat to be rejected for various tool sizes and various machine duty cycles; hence cooling water data is generally arrived at from water measurements from machines installed with mains cooling systems. Temperature rises are invariably small, 10°-15°F generally suffices. Though a machine designer calls for lowest possible water inlet temperatures, cooling tower design performance treated as for refrigeration condenser cooling — or at best, only 5°F closer approach — normally meets requirements.

(f) CHEMICAL AND REFINERY PLANTS

These are too varied to permit of definition. They may be restricted to barometric condensers with close approach, small cooling range and small flow rate or, in major oil refineries, may be for very large flows demanding thoroughly reliable cooling towers. Only in some gas works duties and a few special chemical plants involving small water quantities, is a cooling tower complicated by problems of objectionable compounds, e.g. naphthalene, or corrosion, though a few overseas installations have to function on cooling water which is exceptionally saline.

In all of these plants, however, summer inlet and re-cooled water temperatures are generally fixed by plant designers with precision and the possibility of changing plant water temperatures for more economic towers is seldom practicable.

In some plastic production plants, high water temperatures may be a ruling factor in the selection of type and material for cooling tower packing.

(g) TURBINE CONDENSER COOLING

It is in this field where the largest water flows, the easiest cooling duties and the largest cooling towers are met. In Europe, the easy cooling demanded is met by natural draught towers except in a few exceptional cases where mechanical draught towers are required for reasons of height limitations. In tropical areas, however, steam turbine condenser cooling demands mechanical draught cooling towers for optimum efficiency, for in such situations the natural draught tower is generally unreliable.

Cooling ranges vary between small industrial and giant power station condensers but are between 10°-20°F. Approach temperatures may be 20°-30°F according to locality, of course. In most cases, fogging hazards, from wind-assisted precipitation of the saturated exhaust air, is a special consideration where visibility in public areas and road icing in winter may be possible. These are special risks, of course, with batteries of giant mechanical draught towers, for which there may be additional chances of recirculation — one tower inducing saturated vapour from another tower's exhaust where tower siting is not ideal.

The Ferrybridge, Yorkshire, Power Station Disaster of 1965 has pinpointed the need to determine tower shell height and construction only after the fullest study of disposition of towers on a site and accurate prognosis of gale force wind gusts.

Whether met by natural or mechanical draught cooling towers, turbine condenser cooling is demanded for firmly defined thermal duty at an equally firmly defined air wet bulb temperature, and air dry bulb temperature In Britain, power stations do not have their towers specified principally for summer air conditions as generating stations are fully loaded only in winter In tropical situations, though, some generating stations are fully loaded in high summer on account of large air conditioning and refrigeration demand and here it is appropriate to design condenser and cooling tower operating performance for summer air temperatures.

PLATE 1
A small glass-fibre contra-flow cooling tower.

PLATE 2

Five small glass-fibre cooling towers, each serving a separate cooling system.

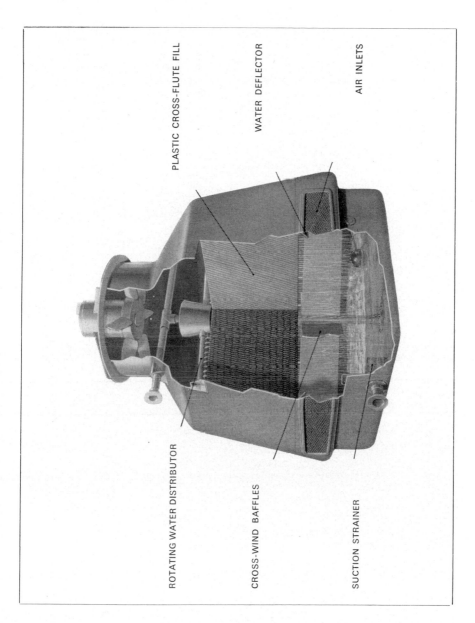

PLASTIC CROSS-FLUTE FILL

WATER DEFLECTOR

AIR INLETS

ROTATING WATER DISTRIBUTOR

CROSS-WIND BAFFLES

SUCTION STRAINER

PLATE 3
A contra-flow all-plastic cooling tower.

By courtesy of Thermotank International Limited

PLATE 4
An induced draught cooling tower with extended tank and connecting pipework.

PLATE 5
A forced draught cooling tower with axial flow fan.

PLATE 6

A twin-cell cooling tower with integral steel basin, mounted on a roof.

PLATE 7
Three large contra-flow cooling towers installed on a hospital roof.

By courtesy of Thermotank International Limited

PLATE 8
A small contra-flow cooling tower with mild steel shell and base
tank.

PLATE 9

A cross-flow cooling tower with glass-fibre shell, plastic packing and axial flow fan.

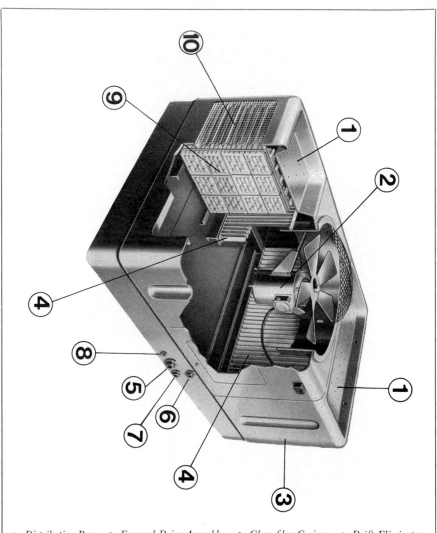

1. *Distribution Pan.*   2. *Fan and Drive Assembly.*   3. *Glass-fibre Casing.*   4. *Drift Eliminators.*
5. *Outlet.*   6. *Overflow.*   7. *Drain.*   8. *Immersion heater connection.*   9. *Plastic packing.*
10. *Air inlet louvres.*

PLATE 10
A cross-flow tower cut away to show internal arrangement.

PLATE 11
A three-cell induced draught contra-flow cooling tower with
integral base tank.

PLATE 12
A contra-flow cooling tower with timber structure, plastic pack and grey 'Galbestos' cladding.

PLATE 13

Two single-cell induced-draught cooling towers installed at a steel works.

PLATE 14

A large single-cell induced draught cooling tower.   Notice the door,
which gives easy access to the distribution system for
maintenance.

PLATE 15
A large single-cell contra-flow cooling tower with three natural draught timber cooling towers in the background.

PLATE 16

A large twin-cell induced draught contra-flow cooling tower. The
stacks on the fan outlets are necessary to prevent steam
interfering with the vision of an overhead-crane-driver.

SECTION 2 — theory

---

chapter 9

PSYCHROMETRY & HEAT TRANSFER THEORY

Definitions
Psychrometric Chart
Total Heat Tables
Wet-bulb Temperature
Heat Transfer Principles

9. Psychrometry & Heat Transfer Theory

The design and selection of cooling towers requires a knowledge of psychrometry, which is the study of the moisture content of air.

Air is composed mainly of oxygen and nitrogen with small quantities of rare gases such as, neon, helium and krypton, and also water vapour in varying quantities depending on its temperature and 'humidity'.

Partial Pressure

Each constituent of air exerts its own individual pressure on its surroundings. These individual pressures are called partial pressures, and it is their sum that we know as atmospheric pressure. The partial pressure is directly proportional to the amount of the gas (% by vol.) present in the mixture. Thus atmospheric air is 80% nitrogen by volume and the partial pressure exerted by the nitrogen is equal to:-

$$\frac{80}{100} \times 14.7 = 11.76 \text{ p.s.i.}$$

Vapour Pressure

Water exerts a pressure at its surface. This pressure is a function of the temperature of the water and is known as vapour pressure. There is a definite relationship between the water temperature and vapour pressure. The values of temperature corresponding to various pressures are set out in steam tables, a portion of which are reproduced in Table 9.

Saturated Air

It is the difference between the vapour pressure of a water surface and the partial pressure of water vapour in the atmosphere which causes evaporation.

Air at a given temperature can absorb a limited amount of water vapour. The higher the temperature, the greater the amount. When it contains this amount it is said to be saturated, and at this condition the partial pressure of the water vapour is equal to the vapour pressure of water at the air temperature.

TABLE 9
Vapour Pressures for Varying Temperatures

Temp. °F.	Pressure Ins. H$_g$.	Temp. °F.	Pressure Ins. H$_g$.	Temp. °F.	Pressure Ins. H$_g$.
34	0.1990	66	0.6441	98	1.8200
36	0.2117	68	0.6902	100	1.9334
38	0.2290	70	0.7392	102	2.0529
40	0.2477	72	0.7911	104	2.1786
42	0.2676	74	0.8463	106	2.3110
44	0.2890	76	0.9047	108	2.4503
46	0.3119	78	0.9667	110	2.5968
48	0.3363	80	1.0323	112	2.7507
50	0.3624	82	1.1017	114	2.9125
52	0.3903	84	1.1752	116	3.0823
54	0.4200	86	1.2530	118	3.2606
56	0.4518	88	1.3351	120	3.4477
58	0.4856	90	1.4219	122	3.6439
60	0.5216	92	1.5136	124	3.8496
62	0.5599	94	1.6103	126	4.0651
64	0.6007	96	1.7124	128	4.2910

Saturation Vapour Pressure
When the air is saturated the vapour pressure is called the saturation vapour pressure.

Absolute Humidity
This is the amount of water vapour contained in air at a given condition. It is usually expressed in lb. of water per lb. of dry air.

Relative Humidity
This is the ratio of water vapour pressure in the air (P), to the saturation vapour pressure (Ps) at the same temperature. It is usually expressed as a percentage: $\left(\text{thus } \% \text{ RH} = \dfrac{100 \text{ P}}{\text{Ps}} \right)$

Dew Point
This is the temperature at which a mixture of air and water vapour becomes saturated.

Dry Bulb Temperature
This is the air temperature, measured in the normal manner by a conventional thermometer.

Wet Bulb Temperature

The wet bulb temperature is so called because it is obtained by causing the air being measured to flow over the wetted bulb of an ordinary thermometer. The bulb is normally wetted by surrounding it with a cloth or wick soaked in water.

When water is exposed to a comparatively large amount of unsaturated air in adiabatic conditions (ie: no heat gained or rejected externally) the water will assume an equilibrium temperature. This temperature is lower than the air dry bulb but higher than the dew point and it is this which is measured by the wet bulb thermometer.

The significance of wet bulb temperature in cooling tower theory and practice is so great that we shall consider the basic theory and practical measurement of wet bulb temperature in greater detail later in this chapter.

Total Heat or Enthalpy

This is the total heat content of air measured from a fixed datum such as o°F. or 32°F. (the latter is usual in U.K.). It is the arithmetical sum of the sensible heats of the air and water vapour, plus the latent heat of vaporisation of the water.

It is a very important property of air and is widely used in calculating cooling tower performance.

Psychrometric Chart

The properties of air and water vapour mixtures can be represented graphically on a single chart referred to as the Psychrometric Chart. The Chart shown (Fig. 44) has been devised by the Institution of Heating & Ventilating Engineers and is reproduced with their kind permission.

In this chart absolute humidities are plotted against dry bulb temperatures, and lines of constant relative humidity and wet bulb temperature are added.

Any point on this chart defines completely the condition of a given sample of air.

The curve marked 100% gives the absolute humidities of saturated air at various temperatures. This curve is called the 'Saturation Line', for obvious reasons.

Mixtures of air and water represented by points to the left of the saturation line cannot ordinarily exist.

Other properties which can be obtained from the chart are, total heat (or enthalpy), wet bulb temperature and dew point temperature.

The use of the chart to obtain these different properties is illustrated in the skeleton diagram of a psychrometric chart shown in Fig. 45.

Note that in order to define precisely the condition of an air-water mixture only two properties need to be known.

For example:-
Wet bulb and Dry bulb temperature.

Fig. 44. Psychrometric Chart.
(Reproduced by kind permission of I.H.V.E.)

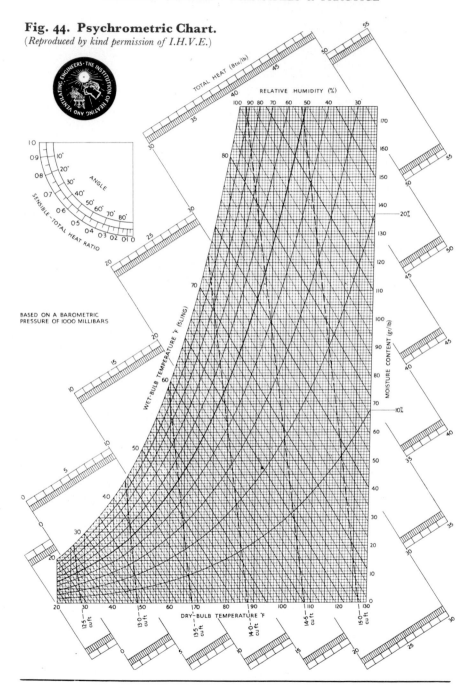

BASED ON A BAROMETRIC
PRESSURE OF 1000 MILLIBARS

Dew point and Dry bulb temperature.

Wet bulb and Dew point temperature.

Enthalpy and Dry bulb temperature.

Absolute humidity and Dry bulb temperature.

Once the point of intersection of two of the above properties has been located on the psychrometric chart, all the other properties can be read off.

Total Heat Tables

Although the psychrometric chart is a very useful tool, the reading of accurate total heats from it is a little inconvenient when carrying out some of the calculations involved in cooling tower design.

It is more convenient therefore to refer to total heat tables and an example of these is given in Table 10. They give the enthalpies of saturated air at various temperatures in 0.1°F. increments.

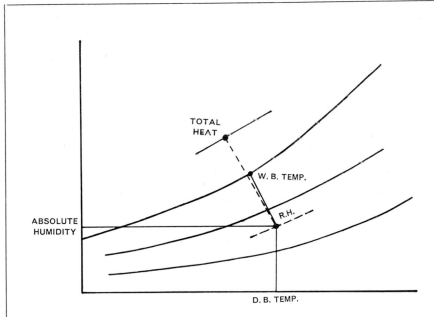

Fig. 45. **Skeleton diagram of Psychrometric Chart.**

TABLE 10

ENTHALPY OF MOIST (SATURATED) AIR (BRITISH UNITS, 32°F. DATUM)

Total pressure: 1 atm.abs (Btu/lb of dry air)

Temp (°F)	0.0	0.1	0.2	0.3	0.4	0.5	0.6	0.7	0.8	0.9
32	4.1	4.2	4.2	4.2	4.3	4.3	4.3	4.4	4.4	4.5
33	4.5	4.6	4.6	4.6	4.7	4.7	4.8	4.8	4.9	4.9
34	4.9	5.0	5.0	5.1	5.1	5.2	5.2	5.2	5.3	5.3
35	5.4	5.4	5.5	5.5	5.5	5.6	5.6	5.7	5.7	5.7
36	5.8	5.8	5.9	5.9	6.0	6.0	6.1	6.1	6.2	6.2
37	6.3	6.3	6.3	6.4	6.4	6.5	6.5	6.6	6.6	6.7
38	6.7	6.7	6.8	6.8	6.9	6.9	7.0	7.0	7.1	7.1
39	7.2	7.2	7.2	7.3	7.3	7.4	7.4	7.5	7.5	7.6
40	7.6	7.7	7.7	7.8	7.8	7.8	7.9	7.9	8.0	8.0
41	8.1	8.1	8.2	8.2	8.3	8.3	8.4	8.4	8.5	8.5
42	8.6	8.6	8.7	8.7	8.8	8.8	8.9	8.9	9.0	9.0
43	9.1	9.1	9.2	9.2	9.3	9.3	9.3	9.4	9.4	9.5
44	9.5	9.6	9.6	9.7	9.7	9.8	9.9	9.9	10.0	10.0
45	10.1	10.1	10.2	10.2	10.3	10.3	10.4	10.4	10.5	10.5
46	10.6	10.6	10.7	10.7	10.8	10.8	10.9	10.9	11.0	11.0
47	11.1	11.1	11.2	11.3	11.3	11.4	11.4	11.5	11.5	11.6
48	11.6	11.7	11.7	11.8	11.8	11.9	11.9	12.0	12.1	12.1
49	12.2	12.2	12.3	12.3	12.4	12.4	12.5	12.6	12.6	12.7
50	12.7	12.8	12.8	12.9	12.9	13.0	13.1	13.1	13.2	13.2
51	13.3	13.3	13.4	13.5	13.5	13.6	13.6	13.7	13.7	13.8
52	13.9	13.9	14.0	14.0	14.1	14.2	14.2	14.3	14.3	14.4
53	14.4	14.5	14.6	14.6	14.7	14.7	14.8	14.9	14.9	15.0
54	15.1	15.1	15.2	15.2	15.3	15.4	15.4	15.5	15.5	15.6
55	15.7	15.7	15.8	15.9	15.9	16.0	16.0	16.1	16.2	16.2
56	16.3	16.3	16.4	16.5	16.5	16.6	16.7	16.7	16.8	16.9
57	16.9	17.0	17.1	17.1	17.2	17.3	17.4	17.4	17.5	17.5
58	17.6	17.7	17.7	17.8	17.8	17.9	18.0	18.0	18.1	18.2
59	18.2	18.3	18.4	18.4	18.5	18.6	18.7	18.7	18.8	18.9
60	18.9	19.0	19.1	19.1	19.2	19.3	19.3	19.4	19.5	19.5
61	19.6	19.7	19.8	19.8	19.9	20.0	20.0	20.1	20.2	20.3
62	20.3	20.4	20.5	20.6	20.6	20.7	20.8	20.8	20.9	21.0
63	21.1	21.1	21.2	21.3	21.4	21.4	21.5	21.6	21.6	21.7
64	21.8	21.9	21.9	22.0	22.1	22.2	22.3	22.3	22.4	22.5
65	22.6	22.6	22.7	22.8	22.9	22.9	23.0	23.1	23.2	23.2
66	23.3	23.4	23.5	23.6	23.6	23.7	23.8	23.9	24.0	24.0
67	24.1	24.2	24.3	24.4	24.4	24.5	24.6	24.7	24.8	24.9
68	24.9	25.0	25.1	25.2	25.3	25.4	25.4	25.5	25.6	25.7
69	25.8	25.9	25.9	26.0	26.1	26.2	26.3	26.4	26.4	26.5
70	26.6	26.7	26.8	26.9	27.0	27.0	27.1	27.2	27.3	27.4

TABLE 10 (continued)

Temp (°F)	0.0	0.1	0.2	0.3	0.4	0.5	0.6	0.7	0.8	0.9
71	27.5	27.6	27.7	27.7	27.8	27.9	28.0	28.1	28.2	28.3
72	28.4	28.5	28.6	28.7	28.7	28.8	28.9	29.0	29.1	29.2
73	29.3	29.4	29.5	29.6	29.7	29.7	29.8	29.9	30.0	30.1
74	30.2	30.3	30.4	30.5	30.6	30.7	30.8	30.9	31.0	31.1
75	31.2	31.3	31.4	31.5	31.6	31.7	31.7	31.8	31.9	32.0
76	32.1	32.2	32.3	32.4	32.5	32.6	32.7	32.8	32.9	33.0
77	33.1	33.2	33.3	33.4	33.5	33.6	33.8	33.9	34.0	34.1
78	34.2	34.3	34.4	34.5	34.6	34.7	34.8	34.9	35.0	35.1
79	35.2	35.3	35.4	35.5	35.6	35.8	35.9	36.0	36.1	36.2
80	36.3	36.4	36.5	36.6	36.7	36.9	37.0	37.1	37.2	37.3
81	37.4	37.5	37.6	37.7	37.8	38.0	38.1	38.2	38.3	38.4
82	38.5	38.6	38.7	38.9	39.0	39.1	39.2	39.3	39.5	39.6
83	39.7	39.8	39.9	40.0	40.1	40.3	40.4	40.5	40.6	40.7
84	40.8	40.9	41.1	41.2	41.3	41.5	41.6	41.7	41.8	42.0
85	42.1	42.2	42.3	42.5	42.6	42.7	42.8	42.9	43.1	43.2
86	43.3	43.4	43.6	43.7	43.8	44.0	44.1	44.2	44.3	44.5
87	44.6	44.7	44.9	45.0	45.1	45.3	45.4	45.5	45.6	45.8
88	45.9	46.0	46.2	46.3	46.4	46.6	46.7	46.8	47.0	47.1
89	47.3	47.4	47.5	47.7	47.8	47.9	48.1	48.2	48.3	48.5
90	48.6	48.7	48.9	49.0	49.2	49.3	49.5	49.6	49.8	49.9
91	50.1	50.2	50.3	50.5	50.6	50.8	50.9	51.1	51.2	51.4
92	51.5	51.7	51.8	52.0	52.1	52.3	52.4	52.6	52.7	52.9
93	53.0	53.2	53.3	53.5	53.6	53.8	53.9	54.1	54.2	54.4
94	54.5	54.7	54.8	55.0	55.1	55.3	55.5	55.6	55.8	55.9
95	56.1	56.3	56.4	56.6	56.7	56.9	57.1	57.2	57.4	57.5
96	57.7	57.9	58.0	58.2	58.4	58.5	58.7	58.9	59.0	59.2
97	59.4	59.5	59.7	59.8	60.0	60.2	60.3	60.5	60.7	60.8
98	61.0	61.2	61.4	61.5	61.7	61.9	62.1	62.2	62.4	62.6
99	62.8	62.9	63.1	63.3	63.5	63.6	63.8	64.0	64.2	64.3
100	64.5	64.7	64.9	65.1	65.3	65.5	65.6	65.8	66.0	66.2
101	66.4	66.6	66.8	67.0	67.2	67.4	67.5	67.7	67.9	68.1
102	68.3	68.5	68.7	68.9	69.1	69.3	69.5	69.7	69.9	70.1
103	70.3	70.4	70.6	70.8	71.0	71.2	71.4	71.6	71.8	72.0
104	72.2	72.4	72.6	72.8	73.1	73.3	73.5	73.7	73.9	74.1
105	74.3	74.5	74.8	75.0	75.2	75.4	75.6	75.8	76.0	76.2
106	76.5	76.7	76.9	77.1	77.3	77.5	77.7	77.9	78.2	78.4
107	78.6	78.8	79.0	79.2	79.4	79.6	79.9	80.1	80.3	80.5
108	80.7	80.9	81.2	81.4	81.7	81.9	82.1	82.4	82.6	82.9
109	83.1	83.3	83.6	83.8	84.1	84.3	84.5	84.8	85.0	85.3
110	85.5	85.7	86.0	86.2	86.5	86.7	86.9	87.2	87.4	87.7
111	87.9	88.1	88.4	88.6	88.9	89.1	89.3	89.6	89.8	90.1
112	90.3	90.6	90.8	91.1	91.4	91.6	91.9	92.2	92.4	92.7
113	93.0	93.2	93.5	93.7	94.0	94.3	94.5	94.8	95.1	95.3
114	95.6	95.9	96.1	96.4	96.7	96.9	97.2	97.5	97.7	98.0

TABLE 10 (continued)

Temp (°F)	0.0	0.1	0.2	0.3	0.4	0.5	0.6	0.7	0.8	0.9
115	98.2	98.5	98.8	99.0	99.3	99.6	99.8	100.1	100.4	100.6
116	100.9	101.2	101.5	101.8	102.1	102.4	102.7	103.0	103.3	103.6
117	103.9	104.2	104.5	104.8	105.1	105.4	105.7	106.0	106.3	106.6
118	106.9	107.1	107.4	107.7	108.0	108.3	108.6	108.9	109.2	109.5
119	109.8	110.0	110.4	110.7	111.0	111.3	111.6	111.9	112.2	112.5
120	112.8	113.1	113.5	113.8	114.1	114.5	114.8	115.1	115.5	115.8
121	116.2	116.5	116.8	117.2	117.5	117.8	118.2	118.5	118.8	119.2
122	119.5	119.8	120.2	120.5	120.8	121.2	121.5	121.8	122.2	122.5
123	122.9	123.2	123.5	123.9	124.2	124.5	124.9	125.2	125.5	125.9
124	126.2	126.6	127.0	127.3	127.7	128.1	128.5	128.8	129.2	129.6
125	130.0	130.3	130.7	131.1	131.5	131.8	132.2	132.6	133.0	133.3
126	133.7	134.1	134.5	134.8	135.2	135.6	136.0	136.3	136.7	137.1
127	137.5	137.8	138.2	138.6	139.0	139.3	139.7	140.1	140.5	140.8
128	141.2	141.6	142.1	142.5	142.9	143.3	143.8	144.2	144.6	145.0
129	145.5	145.9	146.3	146.8	147.2	147.6	148.0	148.5	148.9	149.3
130	149.8	150.2	150.6	151.0	151.5	151.9	152.3	152.7	153.2	153.6
131	154.0	154.5	154.9	155.3	155.7	156.2	156.6	157.0	157.4	157.9
132	158.3	158.8	159.3	159.7	160.2	160.7	161.2	161.7	162.2	162.6
133	163.1	163.6	164.1	164.6	165.1	165.5	166.0	166.5	167.0	167.5
134	168.0	168.4	168.9	169.4	169.9	170.4	170.8	171.3	171.8	172.3
135	172.8	173.3	173.7	174.2	174.7	175.2	175.7	176.2	176.6	177.1

More about Wet Bulb Temperature

As previously mentioned, the wet bulb temperature of air is of such vital importance in cooling tower design that it warrants more detailed treatment.

Suppose that unsaturated air is brought into contact with liquid water under adiabatic conditions (ie: such that no heat is received or given up to the surroundings during the operation). Since the air is not saturated, water will evaporate into it and increase the humidity of the air. The latent heat of evaporation of this water cannot be supplied externally (since, by definition, the process is adiabatic) and, therefore, must be supplied by the cooling of either the air or the water or both.

Consider the case in which a stream of unsaturated air, at constant initial temperature and humidity, is passed over a wetted surface. If the initial temperature of the wetted surface is approximately that of the air, the evaporation of water from the wetted surface tends to lower the temperature of the liquid water.

When the water becomes cooler than the air, sensible heat will be transferred from the air to the water.

Ultimately, an equilibrium will be reached at such a temperature that the loss of heat from the water by evaporation is exactly balanced by the heat passing from the air into the water as sensible heat.

Under such conditions the temperature of the water will remain constant.

This temperature is the wet bulb temperature. If the initial temperature of the wetted surface is below the wet bulb temperature, then it will rise to the wet bulb temperature.

The Measurement of Wet Bulb Temperature

The wet bulb temperature is measured by rapidly passing a stream of air over a mercury-in-glass thermometer, the bulb of which is kept wet by means of a cloth 'sock' either dipped in water or supplied with water.

The SLING PSYCHROMETER is commonly used in determining the wet bulb temperature. In this device two thermometers (one dry bulb thermometer and one wet bulb thermometer) are fastened in a metal frame that can be whirled about a handle.

The psychrometer is whirled for some seconds and the reading of the wet bulb thermometer is observed as quickly as possible. The operation is repeated until successive readings of the wet bulb thermometer show that it has reached its minimum temperature.

The use of this apparatus requires considerable care to obtain reliable results. The operator must ensure that the sock is properly wetted and that the minimum temperature has been reached.

It also requires space enough for the operator to stand and swing the thermometer. This will rarely present a problem in cooling tower practice but can be a serious difficulty in other applications.

Another from of psychrometer uses the same principle but employs a small fan (electric or clockwork). The fan is so small that it can be driven by a dry battery.

The dry cell motor, fan and thermometers can be mounted in a very compact unit. The whole is known as an Aspirated Psychrometer and is sometimes used in precise cooling tower tests. As the velocity of the air is controlled by the speed of the fan, there is no chance, as with the sling psychrometer, of not having a long enough contact time or insufficient air velocity to reach equilibrium.

The Physics of the Process

Let us consider a single drop of water suspended in an atmosphere of unsaturated air, as shown in Fig. 3.

For the moment, we will assume that, as the mass of air is very much greater than the mass of the water, there is no significant change in the condition of the air.

(In practice, of course, and particularly in cooling towers, this is not so and the effect of this change in air condition is an important one as we shall see later).

Surrounding the drop will be a stagnant layer of air known as a 'boundary layer'. Through this film there is diffusing, from the water into the air, W lb. of water vapour per hour. If the latent heat at the wet bulb temperature is λw Btu./lb. the latent heat of the diffusing vapour stream will be λw.W Btu./h.

Also, since the wet bulb temperature is below the temperature of the bulk of the air, sensible heat equal to q Btu./h. will be flowing into the drop.

As wet bulb temperature is an equilibrium temperature, these two streams of heat must be equal, thus:—

$$\lambda w.W = q \qquad \text{Eq.1.}$$

From heat transfer theory, the transfer of sensible heat is equal to the product of three factors — the coefficient of heat transfer, the area of the surface through which the heat is flowing and the temperature difference.

This can be expressed in the following equation:—

$$q = a.\, A\,(t - t_i) \qquad \text{Eq.2.}$$

Where

a = air film heat transfer coefficient (Btu./°F. ft.² h.)

A = the superficial area of the drop (ft.²)

t = bulk air dry bulb temperature (°F.)

t_i = temperature of the water-air interface (°F.)

The rate of transfer of water vapour through the air film surrounding the drop away from the water-air interface by diffusion is given by the equation:—

$$W = K_g.A\,(p_i - p_g) \qquad \text{Eq.3.}$$

Where

W = water diffusing through the air film (lb./h.)

K_g = film coefficient for diffusion and is strictly analogous to the film coefficient for heat transfer $\left(\dfrac{\text{lb.}}{\text{h. ft.}^2\,\text{atm}}\right)$

A = interfacial area (ft.²)

p_i = partial pressure of water vapour at the interface (atm.)

p_g = partial pressure of water vapour in the bulk of the air (atm.)

It is possible and convenient to substitute absolute humidities for the partial pressures in Eq. 3, modifying the constant, of course.

Thus we can write the following equation:—

$$W = K^1_g.A\,(X_i - X_g) \qquad \text{Eq.4.}$$

Where

X_i = absolute humidity of the air at the interface

X_g = absolute humidity of the bulk of the air

In equations 2, 3 and 4 the terms $(t - t_i)$, $(p_i - p_g)$ and $X_i - X_g)$ are referred to as the 'driving force' in each case.

If we substitute the values for q and W from equations 2 and 4 in equation 1, and, as the water temperature at equilibrium is, in fact, the wet bulb temperature of the air, ie: $t_i = t_g$, it follows that:—

$$X_i - X_g = \frac{a\,(t - t_g)}{K^1_g\,\lambda_w} \qquad Eq.5.$$

A very important conclusion can be deduced from the above equation.

As a and K^1_g are coefficients corresponding to the same film, it is reasonable to assume that any influence that tends to change the thickness of the film (and hence the values of the coefficients) will cause the same percentage change in each coefficient.

Therefore, the ratio ($a : K^1_g$) should be independent of such variables as viscosity and air velocity. This has been proved to be so by experiment.

For any value of t and X_g, therefore, there will be a definite value of t_g and X_i that will balance equation 5, as X_i and t_g are co-ordinates of the 100% Relative Humidity (or saturation) Line of the psychrometric chart.

The wet bulb temperature (t_g) (ie: equilibrium temp.) therefore, depends only upon the temperature and humidity of the air and is independent of viscosities, air velocities and other factors which might influence the thickness (and hence resistance) of the air film in contact with the water.

The Heat Transfer Mechanism

The mechanism of the reaction of unsaturated air and water has been explained previously. The process has been shown to be controlled by the flow of heat and diffusion of water vapour through the air film at the interface between air and water.

The conditions at any point in a cooling tower will depend upon whether the temperature of the water is above or below the dry bulb temperature of the air.

When the water temperature is above the dry bulb temperature, as in the upper part of a cooling tower, conditions are as shown in Fig. 46.

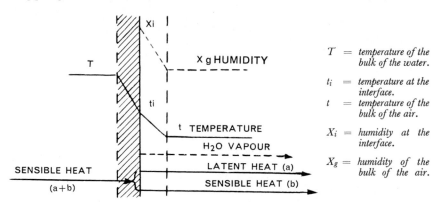

T = temperature of the bulk of the water.

t_i = temperature at the interface.

t = temperature of the bulk of the air.

X_i = humidity at the interface.

X_g = humidity of the bulk of the air.

Fig. 46. Heat transfer with water temperature above dry-bulb temperature.

This diagram is, in effect, a graph, the vertical axis being temperature or absolute humidity, and the horizontal axis representing distance.

The water is being cooled both by evaporation and by the transfer of sensible heat to the air. The humidity and temperature gradients of the air film decrease in the direction of interface to air, and the temperature gradient through the water film $(T - t_i)$ must result in a heat transfer rate high enough to account for both sensible and latent heat loss.

In the parts of the cooling tower where the temperature of the water is higher than that of the wet bulb temperature of the air but below the dry bulb temperature, the conditions will be as shown in Fig. 47.

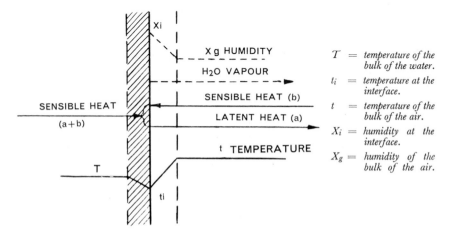

T = temperature of the bulk of the water.
t_i = temperature at the interface.
t = temperature of the bulk of the air.
X_i = humidity at the interface.
X_g = humidity of the bulk of the air.

Fig. 47. Heat transfer with water temperature below dry-bulb temperature but above wet bulb temperature.

Here the water is still being cooled, and the interface will be cooler than the bulk of the water. The temperature gradient will, therefore, be through the water film towards the interface (T is greater than t_i).

However, as the air is being humidified adiabatically, sensible heat must flow from the bulk of the air to the interface (t is greater than t_i).

The sum of heat flowing from the bulk of the water to the interface and from the bulk of the air to the interface results in evaporation. The water vapour thus produced at the interface diffuses through the air film (X_i is greater than X_g).

This flow of water vapour carries away from the interface (as latent heat) all the heat supplied to the interface from both sides.

The latent heat (a) approaches the sensible heat (b) more and more closely as the bottom of the tower is approached. At the bottom of an infinitely tall tower, T would become equal to t_i at the wet bulb temperature of the entering air.

Film Coefficients of Heat Transfer and Diffusion

The rates of heat transfer and diffusion through the air film depend upon the film coefficients a and K^1_g (see page 141). The rate of heat transfer through the water film depends upon the heat transfer coefficient through this film.

It is not practicable to determine these coefficients experimentally, for two reasons. Firstly, it is not possible to measure the temperature of the interface and secondly, the actual contact area between air and water cannot be determined.

The inability to measure t_i can be overcome by basing the driving force on the bulk water and air conditions, modifying the coefficients to suit.

Thus an overall heat transfer coefficient is used based on the difference between the bulk water and air temperatures $(T - t)$.

Similarly, an overall diffusion coefficient based upon the humidity difference $(X_w - X_g)$ where X_w is the saturation humidity corresponding to the bulk water temperature T and X_g is the absolute humidity of the bulk air.

The impossibility of determining the surface area of the air/water interface can be overcome by again modifying the coefficients to refer to a unit volume of the cooling tower packing. The modified coefficients are then known as Volumetric Coefficients.

Factors Influencing the Heat Transfer and Diffusion Coefficients

As both a and K^1_g are film coefficients, each depends primarily upon two factors: first a constant related to the material of the film; second, the thickness of the film.

The first factor is the thermal conductivity, in the case of the heat transfer coefficient, and is the diffusion coefficient in the case of the mass transfer coefficient.

In both cases the thickness of the film is primarily a function of the mass velocity of air passing the film.

chapter 10

HEAT TRANSFER CALCULATIONS

IMPORTANT NOTE

Performance curves and volumetric heat transfer coefficients in this chapter are only illustrative. Numerical values from this chapter should not be used for the design of cooling towers.

10. Heat Transfer Calculations

Quantitative treatment of cooling tower performance by dealing with mass and heat transfer separately is very laborious. Therefore the simplifying approximation of Merkel's total heat theory has been almost universally adopted for the calculation of tower performance.

Briefly, Merkel's theory states that all of the heat transfer taking place at any position in the cooling tower is proportional to the difference between the total heat of the air at that point in the tower, and the total heat of air saturated at the temperature of the water at that point in the tower.

As an equation, the above statement would be written:

$$Q = K.S. (H_w - H_g)$$

Where: Q = Heat transferred by convection and evaporation.

       K = Heat transfer coefficient.

       S = Area of contact between air and water.

       H_w = Enthalpy of air saturated at water temperature.

       H_g = Enthalpy of ambient air.

For Merkel's theory to have a practical value two difficulties have to be overcome.

Firstly, the area of the water surface cannot be determined, but as previously explained, this is overcome by combining K and S in one coefficient K_gS which refers to unit volume of the pack.

Secondly, the above equation refers only to a single point on the pack, whereas water and air conditions vary throughout the tower.

It is necessary, therefore, to use the mean value of enthalpy difference, and this is referred to as the Mean Driving Force.

A convenient way of showing driving force graphically is to plot total heats of the air mass and air film against tower position as shown in Fig. 48.

Note that the tower 'Mean Position' is that position at which the water temperature is the arithmetic mean of the inlet and outlet water temperatures. In fact, sometimes water temperatures are taken as the horizontal scale. In these cases it is important to remember that air temperatures cannot be read off this scale.

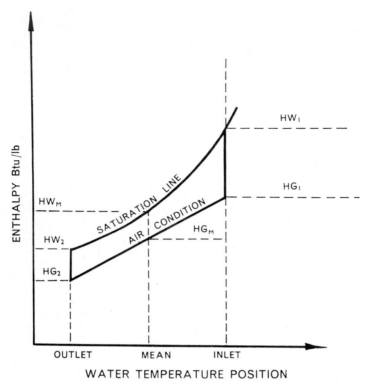

Fig. 48. A convenient way of showing enthalpy differences is by the driving force diagram.

The thin film of air surrounding the water droplets or particles is always saturated and, therefore, the water line will have a shape similar to the saturation curve of the Psychrometric Chart.

If we consider the heat balance between water and air we have:—

$$L.td = G \, (H_{g1} - H_{g2}) \qquad \text{Eq. 1.}$$

Where: L = the water flow rate (lb./h.)

td = temperature range through which the water is to be cooled (°F.)

G = the air flow rate (lb./h.)

H_{g2} = the enthalpy of the inlet air (Btu./lb.)

H_{g1} = the enthalpy of the outlet air (Btu./lb.)

This equation may be re-written:

$$H_{g1} = \frac{L.td}{G} + H_{g2} \qquad \text{Eq. 2.}$$

This is a linear equation, and therefore the air line on the driving force diagram will always be a straight line.

The vertical distance between the two graphs gives the difference in enthalpies (or driving force) at any cross-section through the packing.

The mean value of these driving forces (Mean Driving Force) may be found by using a chart devised by W. L. Stevens for this purpose.

The chart shown in Fig. 49 uses the difference in enthalpies at the top and bottom of the tower, and also at the tower 'Mean Position'.

We can now re-write our basic equation:—

$$E_t = K_gS. \; l.a. \; \triangle H_m \qquad \qquad \text{Eq. 3.}$$

Where: $\triangle H_m$ is the Mean Driving Force $\quad l = $ height of packing.
$a = $ horizontal cross-sectional area of packing.

E_t, the total amount of heat transferred in the pack, is also equal to the product of liquid flow rate and cooling range, or L.td, so that we can write:

$$E_t = L.td = K_gS. \; l.a. \; \triangle H_m \qquad \text{Eq. 4.}$$

$$\text{or, by re-arranging:} \quad K_gS = \frac{L.td}{l.a. \cdot \triangle H_m} \quad \text{Eq. 5.}$$

It follows that, as the total amount of heat transferred is also equal to the product of the air flow rate and the difference between initial and final air enthalpies: $G. \; (H_{g1} - H_{g2})$ then:—

$$K_gS = \frac{G \; (H_{g1} - H_{g2})}{l.a. \; \triangle H_m} \qquad \qquad \text{Eq. 6.}$$

It should be noted that the above equation assumes that L and G are constant, whereas, of course, evaporation takes place. At normal temperature levels this does not result in any significant error.

Calculation of Mean Driving Force

Let us assume we wish to calculate the Mean Driving Force when given the following information:—

$H_{g2} = $ Enthalpy of air entering tower (Btu./lb.)

$L = $ Water flow rate through tower (lb./h.)

$G = $ Air flow rate through tower (lb./h.)

$t_{w1} = $ Water temperature entering tower (°F.)

$t_{w2} = $ Water temperature leaving tower (°F.)

We can calculate:—

Water temperature difference: $td = t_{w2} - t_{w1}$

Enthalpy of air at Mean Tower Position: $H_{gm} = \dfrac{H_{g1} + H_{g2}}{2}$

We can construct our driving force diagram as follows:—

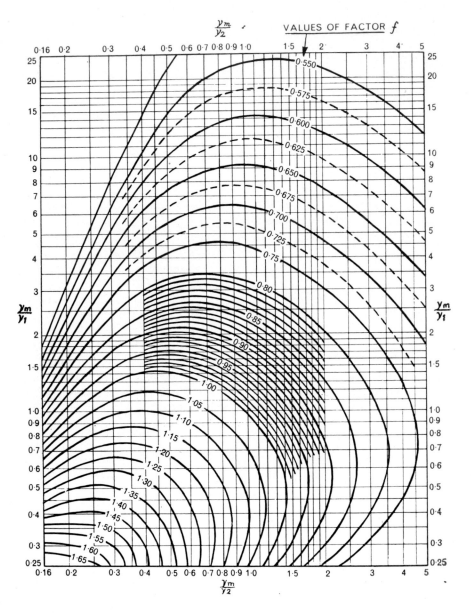

Fig. 49. Chart for determination of mean driving force.

(*By Carey & Williamson, based upon a chart prepared by W. L. Stevens*).

Plot enthalpy for various temperatures from the tables commencing on page 136 to obtain the water side curve, noting the value of H_{wm}.

Plot the line representing the air side condition by joining the points representing H_{g1} and H_{g2}. (Once one has become familiar with the principles involved, the actual construction of the driving force diagram is unnecessary).

We now find the three driving forces:

$(H_{w1} - H_{g1}) = Y_1$ (At the top of the tower)

$(H_{wm} - H_{gm}) = Y_m$ (At the tower mean position)

$(H_{w2} - H_{g2}) = Y_2$ (At the bottom of the tower)

The ratios $\dfrac{Y_m}{Y_1}$ and $\dfrac{Y_m}{Y_2}$ are now calculated and the value of the factor 'f' found from the Stevens chart in Fig. 49.

Mean Driving Force is then found from:

$$\triangle H_m = f.Y_m = f.(H_{wm} - H_{gm})$$

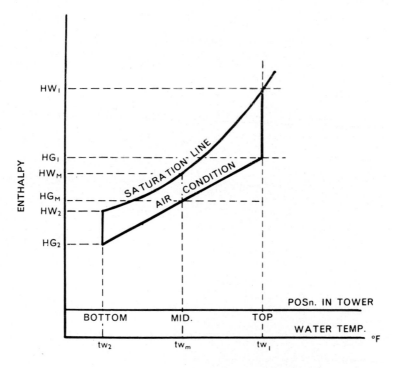

Fig. 50. Driving force diagram.

THE VOLUME TRANSFER COEFFICIENT

Having calculated the mean driving force, it is necessary to know the value of the volume transfer coefficient K_gS, before a prediction of tower performance can be made.

Any single value of K_gS will apply to only one set of conditions, i.e. water and air flow rates and type of packing.

The manufacturer of the packing will usually obtain, experimentally, values of K_gS for varying values of $\left(\dfrac{L}{a}\right)$ and $\left(\dfrac{G}{a}\right)$ ie: for values of air and water flow rates per unit of cross-sectional area of packing. These experimental results are usually expressed in a formula which takes the form:—

$$K_gS = C.\left(\frac{L}{a}\right)^m\left(\frac{G}{a}\right)^n$$

Where C, m and n are constants for the pack tested.

Given this equation, therefore, a value of K_gS can be found for any values of $\left(\dfrac{L}{a}\right)$ and $\left(\dfrac{G}{a}\right)$

SELECTION OF TOWER SIZE FOR A GIVEN DUTY

Now we can look at the steps to be taken in selecting a tower for a given duty. This involves a 'trial and error' method.

The information required would be:—

1. Inlet water temperature.

2. Outlet water temperature.

3. Water flow rate.

4. Design ambient air condition.

5. Air flow rate per unit of horizontal cross-sectional area of pack.

6. The values of the constants in the equation $K_gS = C.\left(\dfrac{L}{a}\right)^m\left(\dfrac{G}{a}\right)^n$

Usually items 1, 2 and 3 are fixed by the user and are dictated mainly by the process.

The ambient condition will depend on the geographical location of the site, and a design figure is arrived at after referring to relevant meteorological data, including atmospheric pressure change for localities well above sea level (see later text).

5 and 6 will be fixed by the tower manufacturer. Usually a value of $\left(\dfrac{G}{a}\right)$ is decided upon for practical reasons, ie: to limit pressure drop and prevent carry-over.

Step 1.

Assume the cross-sectional area of the packing.

Step 2.

Determine K_gS from $\left(\dfrac{L}{a}\right)$ and $\left(\dfrac{G}{a}\right)$

Step 3.

Calculate $\triangle H_m$

Step 4.

Calculate K_gS from: $K_gS = \dfrac{L.td}{l.a.\triangle H_m}$

Step 5.

Compare the values of K_gS obtained in Steps 2 and 4. If these do not agree, the assumption made in Step 1 was incorrect and the process should be repeated using a new value of a.

It should be noted that the method outlined above, including the use of the Stevens chart, applies only to contra-flow towers. A different method (which is beyond the scope of this book) applies to cross-flow towers.

In addition, the above method assumes that the packing height is known. This is often fixed at a standard dimension in the case of small industrial towers, although variations in height of packing are very usual when designing large cooling towers.

Example

A cooling tower is required for the jacket cooling of a Diesel Engine. 20,000 gph of water at 90°F. on to the jacket is required, leaving at 120°F. A design air wet bulb temperature of 65°F. is to be used.

The packing specification is:—

Air flow rate: 1,600 lb./h.ft.^{2}; $K_gS = 30\left(\dfrac{L}{a}\right)^{0.2}\left(\dfrac{G}{a}\right)^{0.27}$

For a packing height of 2 ft. what is the area of the tower required?

Step 1.

Assume cross-sectional area of 80 ft.^{2}

This is a reasonable figure for the application, and unfortunately, there is no alternative to experience in making a reasonably accurate first guess.

Step 2.

Determine K_gS from $\left(\dfrac{L}{a}\right)$ and $\left(\dfrac{G}{a}\right)$

$K_gS = 30 \times \left(\dfrac{200,000}{80}\right)^{0.2} \times \left(\dfrac{1,600}{1}\right)^{0.27} = 1,050$

Step 3.

Calculate $\triangle H_m$

$$H_{g1} = H_{g2} + \frac{L.td}{G}$$

$$= 22.6 + \frac{200,000 \times (120\text{-}90)}{1,600 \times 80}$$

$$= 69.5 \text{ Btu./lb. dry air.}$$

$$H_{gm} = \frac{H_{g1} + H_{g2}}{2}$$

$$= \frac{69.5 + 22.6}{2}$$

$$= 46.1 \text{ Btu./lb. dry air.}$$

The enthalpy values related to the water temperatures 120°F., 105°F. and 90°F. are found from the enthalpy tables and can be inserted in the driving force diagram as shown (Fig. 51).

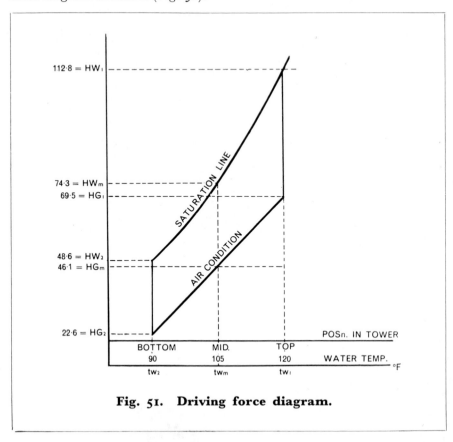

Fig. 51. **Driving force diagram.**

$$Y_1 = (H_{w1} - H_{g1}) \quad = (112.8 - 69.5) = 43.3$$
$$Y_m = (H_{wm} - H_{gm}) \quad = (\ 74.3 - 46.1) = 28.2$$
$$Y_2 = (H_{w2} - H_{g2}) \quad = (\ 48.6 - 22.6) = 26.0$$

$$\frac{Y_m}{Y_1} = \frac{28.2}{43.3} = 0.653 \qquad \text{also} \qquad \frac{Y_m}{Y_2} = \frac{28.2}{26.0} = 1.082$$

From the Stevens Chart Fig. 49, the factor 'f' = 1.045.

Mean Driving Force; $\triangle H_m = 29.5$ Btu./lb. dry air.

Step 4.

$$K_g S = \frac{L.td}{l.a.\triangle H_m} = \frac{200,000 \times 30}{2 \times 80 \times 29.5} = 1,265$$

Step 5.

The two values for $K_g S$ which we have found are 1,265 and 1,050. The difference in these is too great for the original assumption of 80 sq. ft. to be considered acceptable.

We must make a new assumption, therefore, and as the value of $K_g S$ found in Step 4 is greater than that in Step 2, a larger area must be considered.

If we repeat the above series of calculations assuming 90 sq. ft., the respective values of $K_g S$ will be 1,040 and 1,032. These are sufficiently close for the assumption of 90 sq. ft. to be accepted.

A similar series of calculations can be made to predict the performance for a given tower size. In this case the information given will be:—

1. Dimensions of the packing.

2. Air flow rate.

3. Performance details of the packing.

4. Ambient air conditions.

The remaining variables are:—inlet and outlet water temperatures and the water flow rate. Two of these are normally fixed, and the problem is to find the third. For example, if water enters the tower at a certain flow rate and temperature, what will be the re-cooled temperature?

Again a trial and error method is needed, the steps being:—

Step 1.

Assume an 'off' temperature.

Step 2.

Calculate $\triangle H_m$.

Step 3.

Calculate $K_g S$ from: $K_g S = \dfrac{L.td}{l.a.\ \triangle H_m}$

Step 4.

Calculate K_gS from: $K_gS = C. \left(\dfrac{L}{a}\right)^m \left(\dfrac{G}{a}\right)^n$

Step 5.

Compare the values of K_gS from (3) and (4). If these do not agree, repeat the series of calculations using a new value of re-cooled water temperature.

Example:

A cooling tower has been installed having the following characteristics:

(a)   Horizontal cross-sectional area..   ..   ..   45 sq. ft.

(b)   Packing height ..   ..   3 ft.

(c)   Design water flow rate ..   ..   9,000 gph

(d)   Air flow rate   ..   ..   80,000 lb./h.

(e) K_gS at the design air and water flow rates   ..   2,470

What would be the re-cooled water temperature if the inlet temperature were 100°F. and the ambient air wet bulb temperature 68°F.?

Step 1.

Assume an 'off' temperature of 75°F.

Step 2.

$\triangle H_m$, the Mean Driving Force, is found as before:

$$H_{g1} = H_{g2} + \frac{L.td}{G} = 24.9 + \frac{90,000}{80,000}(100-75) = \begin{array}{c} 53.0 \text{ Btu./lb.} \\ \text{dry air.} \end{array}$$

$$H_{gm} = \frac{H_{g1} + H_{g2}}{2} = \frac{53.0 + 24.9}{2} = 38.9 \text{ Btu./lb. dry air.}$$

The driving force diagram can be constructed. (Fig. 52).

$Y_1 = (H_{w1} - H_{g1}) \quad = \quad 11.5$

$Y_m = (H_{wm} - H_{gm}) \quad = \quad 6.4$

$Y_2 = (H_{w2} - H_{g2}) \quad = \quad 6.3$

$\dfrac{Y_m}{Y_1} = 0.557 \qquad \dfrac{Y_m}{Y_2} = 1.016$

From the Stevens chart, factor 'f' = 1.05 (Fig. 41).

Mean Driving Force = $\triangle H_m$ = 1.05 × 6.4 = 6.72 Btu./lb. dry air.

Step 3.

$$K_gS = \frac{90,000 \times 25}{3 \times 45 \times 6.72} = 2,480$$

Step 4.

K_gS is given as 2,470.

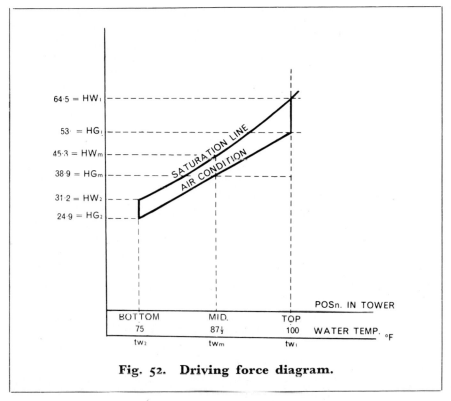

Fig. 52. Driving force diagram.

Step 5.

The difference between the values of K_gS found in Steps 3 and 4 is small enough for the original assumption of 75°F. water 'off' temperature to be considered correct.

Corrections for Altitude

The psychrometric chart given in Fig. 44, was prepared on the basis of an atmospheric pressure of 1,000 millibars. When the atmospheric pressure differs from this, the chart ceases to be completely accurate.

For small changes in pressure the error is small, but where there are appreciably lower pressures, as at high altitudes, then it is necessary to apply a correction.

The total heat of air, at a particular dry bulb temperature and absolute humidity, is independent of barometric pressure. However, the moisture carrying ability of the air is increased with reduced pressure, and the composition of the air/water vapour mixture at saturation changes.

Total heat at saturation, therefore, will increase with altitude as shown in Fig. 53. In the chart, the increase in total heat is shown for various saturation temperatures against barometric pressure.

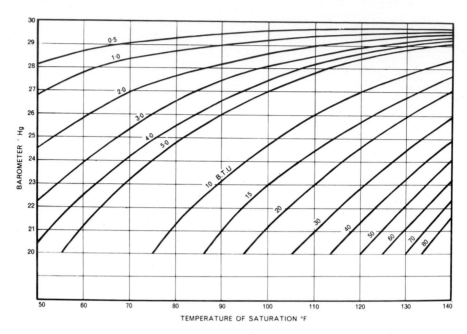

Fig. 53. Increase in enthalpy for reduced barometric pressure.

TABLE 11

Altitude factors

Altitude relative to sea level	Barometric pressure In. Hg.	Relative Density at DB Temperature		
		30°F.	60°F.	90°F.
1,000 ft. below	31.2	1.10	1.04	0.984
Sea Level	30.0	1.060	1.000	0.945
1,000 ft. above	28.9	1.022	0.964	0.911
2,000 ,, ,,	27.9	0.986	0.930	0.879
3,000 ,, ,,	26.9	0.951	0.896	0.847
4,000 ,, ,,	25.9	0.916	0.864	0.816
5,000 ,, ,,	25.0	0.884	0.832	0.786
6,000 ,, ,,	24.0	0.850	0.801	0.757
8,000 ,, ,,	22.3	0.788	0.743	0.702
10,000 ,, ,,	20.6	0.730	0.688	0.650
15,000 ,, ,,	16.9	0.599	0.564	0.533

The relationship between altitude and barometric pressure is shown in Table 11.

The effect of the increase in total heat is to improve the driving force and so tend to reduce the size of tower needed for a particular duty. However, this is counteracted by the fan delivering a smaller mass of air due to the reduced density of the air (the fan being a 'constant volume machine'). With the relative density of air at 30″ HG and 60°F DB being taken as unity, the relative densities at other temperatures and barometric pressures are shown in Table 11.

The heat transfer calculations for a tower to operate at a higher altitude are as shown in the previous example, once the total heats and mass flow of air have been corrected.

Use of Selection Charts

As the examples in this Chapter show, the determination of tower size for a given duty can be a tedious process.

Cooling tower manufacturers who are faced with this problem many times each day prepare charts to make selection easier. Large numbers of calculations are made and the results plotted in graphical form.

The selection graphs or charts can take many forms, but a typical example is shown in Fig. 54, being the data relating to a type of plastic film packing. In this case each chart is drawn for a constant air wet bulb temperature. Water flow rates per square foot of packing cross-section are represented by the vertical axis and water 'on' temperature on the horizontal axis. Lines of constant re-cooled water temperature are plotted.

Use of the chart is a very simple matter. For the specified air wet bulb temperature, and given water 'on' and 'off' temperatures and flow rate the value of $\left(\dfrac{W}{a}\right)$ can be read off directly. $\left(\dfrac{W}{a} \times 10 = \dfrac{L}{a}\right)$

The tower size is found by dividing the total water flow rate by this value.

Example:

In an air-conditioning plant, 1,000,000 Btu./h. are to be dissipated from the condenser. 10,000 gph of water is to be used, the temperatures on and off the condenser being 75°F. and 85°F. respectively. For a design air wet bulb temperature of 65°F., what tower size is required?

Referring to the selection chart, Fig. 55, the intersection of the 85°F. water 'on' line with the 75°F. water 'off' line shows a flow rate per ft.² of 235 gph.

The tower area is therefore $\dfrac{10,000}{235} = 42.5$ ft.²

Selection charts can also be used to predict cooling tower performance under varying conditions.

The previous example was where a condenser dissipated 1,000,000 Btu./h. when circulating 10,000 gph, the water temperature being 85°F. and 75°F.

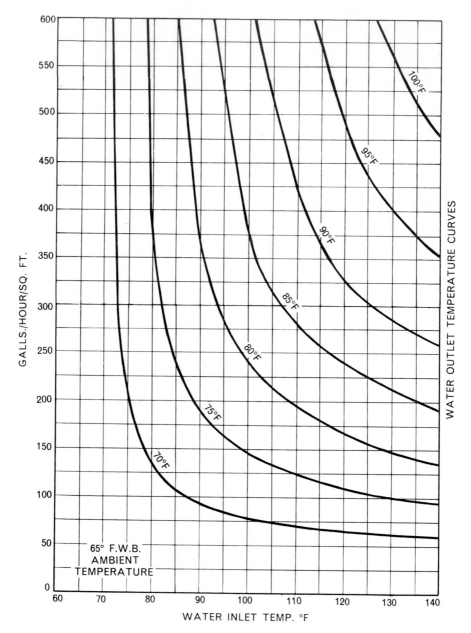

Fig. 54. Cooling tower selection chart 65°F. Wet Bulb.

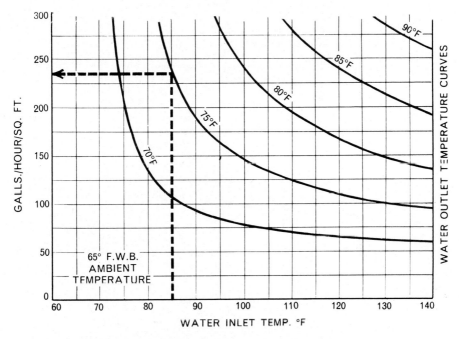

Fig. 55. **Cooled from 85°F. to 75°F. at 65°F.W.B. needs 235 gph per ft.²**

For the design air wet bulb temperature of 65°F. the tower area from the charts was 42.5 ft.².

Should the condenser tubes become scaled, restricting flow while the heat dissipation remains virtually constant, the water temperatures must also change to compensate.

In our example, if the water flow rate changes to 8,330 gph we can find the new temperature as follows:—

The new temperature difference will be:—

$$t_d = \frac{\text{Heat dissipation}}{\text{Water flow rate}} = \frac{1,000,000}{8,330 \times 10} = 12°F.$$

We must construct a 'Constant Temperature Difference' line on the selection chart. By adding 12°F. to each re-cooled water temperature line we can find the corresponding tower inlet water temperature and the intersection of each tower inlet water ordinate with the appropriate re-cooled water curve gives a point on our new curve. (Fig. 56).

The flow rate per unit area of tower will now be:—

$$\frac{W}{a} = \frac{\text{Total water flow rate}}{\text{Cross-sectional area}} = \frac{8,330}{42.5} = 196 \text{ gph/ft.}^2$$

The intersection of the 196 gph/ft.² line with the 12°F. temperature

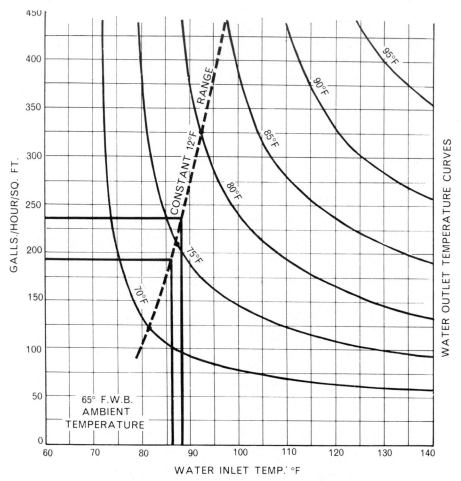

Fig. 56. The 'Constant Temperature Difference' line helps to determine varying performance.

difference line will, therefore, give the new operating conditions.

Thus the water inlet and re-cooled temperatures are found to be 86°F. and 74°F. respectively.

Another variation occurring in practice, is when the cooling load is greater than the design figure. In our example, if the load increased to 1,200,000 Btu./h., with the flow rate of 10,000 gph, obviously, the temperatures must change to compensate.

The modified temperature difference is again 12°F., and we can use the curve constructed in the last example. The intersection of the 235 gph/ft.² line with this curve gives the new water temperatures which are found to be 88°F. and 76°F. 'on' and 'off' respectively.

Now that we have seen how tower performance will vary to meet conditions let us look at the effect of this on selection.

For example, in the case of the condenser, if the flow rate is halved and temperature range doubled, the heat dissipation is still 1,000,000 Btu./h. For the same design air wet bulb temperature, the tower size from the selection chart is found from the unit area flow rate corresponding to the selected temperature.

With the same re-cooled water temperature as before, 75°F., the water inlet temperature is 95°F. and the unit flow rate will be 162.6 gph/ft.².

$$\text{Tower area required} = \frac{5,000}{162.5} = 30.8 \text{ ft.}^2$$

Had we changed the level of the temperatures slightly to say 100°F. and 80°F., the tower area required would be half of the original selection, ie: 21.3 ft.².

It can be seen, therefore, that for a given cooling load the size of tower will vary considerably depending on four factors:—

1. The design air wet bulb temperature selected.

2. The temperature range.

3. The approach.

4. The water flow rate.

Naturally, flow rates and temperatures cannot be altered without careful consideration, but there are many cases where the most economical tower is not selected.

In the example given above, variations in water temperatures and flow rate have a considerable effect on the performance of the compressor of the refrigeration plant, and departure from design is not recommended without the manufacturer's approval. It may well be that relatively small alterations to the condenser design can reduce the tower size considerably, giving an overall saving. This is a point which is often overlooked when designing a refrigeration system.

In many industrial applications, temperatures are not so critical and careful selection of water temperatures and flow rates can result in considerable savings.

To illustrate this point let us again take an example and study the effect of varying conditions. This time we will consider a quenching process where the heat dissipation rate is 1,000,000 Btu./h.

As before, with a circulation of 10,000 gph and water temperatures of 85°F. 'on', and 75°F. 'off', the tower size for 65°F. air wet bulb temperature is 42.5 ft.².

If the water temperatures are increased to 95°F. and 85°F. with the same dissipation rate and air wet bulb temperature, the tower size is now 19.1 ft.²

In the case illustrated, it is unlikely that this comparatively small rise in the temperature of the quenching medium will be of any consequence, unless the quenching medium is oil and a shell and tube heat exchanger is being used. If this is so, it will of course, be necessary to find the economic balance between cooling tower and heat exchanger size.

Average design air wet bulb temperatures for air-conditioning and refrigeration applications in the British Isles.

chapter 11

DETERMINATION OF WATER COOLING DUTIES

11. Determination of Water Cooling Duties

One of the most important aspects of cooling system design is the determination of the water cooling duty. This is fundamental because it determines the size (and possibly type) of cooling tower that should be used.

Consequently, before the cooling duty can be established, it is necessary to establish data concerning the water flow rate and the upper and lower temperature limits of the water passing through the plant being cooled.

Guidance on the general principles involved and some data for specific types of water-cooled equipment are given in other parts of this book. The reader can refer to the section on 'Determination of Duty' in Chapter 4 and to the various descriptions of industrial applications in Chapter 8.

The object of this chapter is to describe the principles involved in rather more detail.

Water Flow Rate

This depends mostly upon: the permissible water temperature rise, necessity to limit pumping head and the need to induce heat transfer within the equipment being cooled.

Generally, the engineer installing equipment is given recommended water flow rates by the manufacturer. These tend to be maxima rather than minima and careful questioning sometimes results in a reduction in the flow rate specified.

Cooled Equipment Inlet Water Temperature

The necessary water temperature to the cooled equipment (which is, of course, the same as the re-cooled water temperature from the cooling tower outlet) for a given heat dissipation rate, depends upon: the temperature levels of the process being cooled, the amount of cooled surface and the effectiveness of the heat transfer between cooled surfaces and the cooling water.

A crucial factor is the required temperature of the cooled surfaces. The cooling water must not only enter the equipment at a lower temperature than the process but cannot rise above it in passing through the equipment.

As explained in Chapter 4, the theoretical minimum to which water can be cooled by an evaporative cooling tower is the ambient air wet bulb temperature. A typical design air wet bulb temperature for industrial processes in the U.K. is 60°F. Evaporative cooling towers can be designed to cool within a few degrees of the air wet bulb temperature but for reasons of capital and running costs are not usually designed for off-water temperatures below 70°F and a very common off-water temperature is 75°F.

If water temperatures much below 70°F are required, then it is necessary to use refrigeration equipment. This is a decision which should be considered very carefully before being taken. Indeed, the much greater capital, running and maintenance costs of refrigeration as compared with air blast or evaporative water coolers constitute a great deterrent to its use. Nevertheless, for some processes (for example, air conditioning) the use of refrigeration is essential and the extra costs must be accepted. (For the same heat dissipation rate, the capital cost of refrigeration equipment for cooling water to, say, 50°F, using mechanical refrigeration, is about eight times more than for an evaporative cooling tower cooling water to about 70°F.).

Water Temperature Rise

The water temperature rise through the cooled equipment, for a given water flow rate, depends upon the heat dissipation to the water from the equipment being cooled. This is the part of the problem which often presents difficulties, and it is not uncommon for the engineer, once he knows the water temperature to the cooled equipment, to decide upon a flow rate and then arrive at a temperature rise by guesswork. For example, having decided that the inlet water temperature should be 75°F, guesses of water temperature rises of 30°F or 40°F seem to be popular, often in cases where the actual temperature rise may be only 10°F or even 5°F. Obviously, such methods will result in cooling towers much larger and more expensive than necessary.

There are various methods, well within the grasp of most engineers, of arriving at reasonably close estimates of heat dissipation using fundamental principles.

In some cases of standard equipment, the manufacturer can give accurate figures, but it is surprising how often the equipment manufacturer is very vague on such matters. This is because, in the past, the manufacturer, frequently, has merely recommended that a particular flow rate of mains water is necessary and has not had occasion to determine the actual heat dissipation. If the heat dissipation rate can be determined from reliable data or by calculation then the water temperature rise follows from the following simple relationship:

$$t_d = \frac{Q}{L} \qquad \text{Eq. 1}$$

where: t_d = Temperature rise of cooling water °F.
Q = Rate of heat dissipation in Btu/h.
L = Rate of flow of cooling water in lb/h.

To obtain reasonably accurate assessments of the rate at which heat will be dissipated to the cooling water, it is necessary to determine it either by a theoretical analysis using the fundamental principles of energy conservation, or to use reliable sources of data on the particular equipment under consideration.

Calculation of Rates of Heat Dissipation

The question that must first be asked when facing this problem is "where is the heat coming from?" The answer will be one of the following four possibilities:

(a) Sensible heat given up due to a fall in temperature of a material being cooled.

(b) Latent heat given up by a material changing phase, i.e. a gas changing to a liquid (latent heat of condensation) or a liquid changing to a solid (latent heat of fusion).

(c) Mechanical power changing to heat as a result of friction between a fluid and a solid or turbulence within a fluid, or, of course, between two solids.

(d) Electrical power changing to heat as a result of electrical resistance in solids or liquids.

In some processes more than one of the above possibilities may occur in one piece of equipment. The method of calculation in each case is as follows:

(a) *Sensible heat from a material being cooled is given by:*
$$Q = M.s \ (t_h - t_c) \qquad \text{Eq. 2}$$
where: Q = Heat dissipation rate in Btu/h.
M = Material flow rate in lb/h.
s = Material specific heat in Btu/lb °F.
t_h = Hot material temperature in °F.
t_c = Cold material temperature in °F.

(b) *Latent heat from a material changing phase is given by:*
$$Q = M.B. \qquad \text{Eq. 3}$$
where: B is the Latent Heat of Condensation in Btu/lb.
$$Q = M.F. \qquad \text{Eq. 4}$$
where: F is the Latent Heat of Fusion in Btu/lb.

(c) *Mechanical power conversion is the rate at which heat is produced from the degradation of mechanical energy and is given by:*
$$Q = 2,545 \times hp \qquad \text{Eq. 5}$$
where: hp is the mechanical power in horsepower.

(d) *Electrical power conversion is the rate at which heat is produced from the degradation of electrical energy and is given by:*
$$Q = 3,412 \times kW \qquad \text{Eq. 6}$$
where: kW = electrical power in kilowatts.

Practical Applications

(a) Sensible and latent heat: In cases where the flow rate of the liquid, gas or solid and the conditions at the beginning and end of the cooling process are known, the application of Equations 2, 3 or 4 will give precisely the rate of heat loss and it can be assumed that all the heat lost will enter the cooling water, i.e. in effect, this is merely the application of a simple heat balance.

b) Power conversion: Equations 5 and 6 are applied to those processes where the source of the heat is power input, either mechanical or electrical. For example, if some machinery is carrying out an operation on a material, such as grinding or rolling, it is a safe assumption that nearly all the motor hp will be converted to heat which will appear in the cooling water. Equation 5 gives the rate at which the heat will enter the cooling system. If the power input is electrical (as, for example, in an anodising tank) one merely applies Equation 6.

Obviously, in both the above examples all the heat or power input will not ultimately appear in the cooling water. However, in most cases it will be quite a high percentage and the system design engineer may well be content to accept the figures calculated from the above methods, secure in the knowledge that he has, in doing so, allowed a safety margin. (This is a sound practice in cooling system design as the various parts of the system can, on occasions, be operating at less than maximum efficiency).

If, however, the design engineer wishes to reduce spare system capacity to the bare minimum, then he must be prepared to submit the cooled equipment to a detailed heat transfer analysis. This would involve tracing the various routes by which the heat or energy input to the equipment can escape to the surroundings and thus not enter the cooling water. He will then need to calculate the rates at which this occurs. In certain types of equipment heat or energy can be absorbed in changing the chemical nature of material and this could also be allowed for.

appendix

SOURCES OF FURTHER INFORMATION

The Industrial Cooling Tower	K. K. McKelvey & Maxey Brooke Elsevier Publishing Co.
Cooling Towers	J. D. Gurney & I. A. Cotter Maclaren & Sons Ltd.
Heat Transmission	McAdams McGraw Hill Book Co.
Process Heat Transfer	Kern McGraw Hill Book Co.
Evaporative Cooling of Circulating Water	L. D. Berman Pergamon Press
Absorption, Distillation and Cooling Towers	W. S. Norman Longmans
Evaporative Water Cooling Equipment	1965 I.H.V.E. Guide to Current Practice
New Trends in Cooling Tower Design Methods and Materials of Construction	D. J. Tow — British Chemical Engineering. March/April 1960
Evaluated Weather Data for Cooling Equipment Design	Head Wrightson Processes Ltd.
Timber Decay and its Control	Forest Products Research Leaflet No. 38: H.M.S.O. Code No. 46-214-39
Model Water By-laws	H.M.S.O.
C.T.I. Code Standard Specifications and Technical Bulletins	Cooling Tower Institute 1120 West 43rd Street, Houston, Texas
Water Treatment Problems in Heating and Ventilating Systems	C. O. Smith J.I.H.V.E. March 1962
Gas Cooling and Humidification Design of Packed Towers from Small Scale Tests	Carey & Williamson Vol. 163 1950 Trans. Ins. Mech. Engs.
Working Stresses for Structural Timbers	Bulletin No. 47 Forest Products Research
The Performance of Grid Packed Towers	W. S. Norman Trans. Ins. Chem. Engs. Vol. 29/1951
Elimination of Carry Over from Packed Towers	H. Chilton Trans. Inst. Chem. Engs. Vol. 30/1952
Simultaneous Heat and Mass Transfer in Cooling Towers	W. J. Thomas & P. Houston British Chemical Engineering, March 1961
Specification for Water Cooling Towers	British Standard 4485. Parts 1 and 2

SYMBOLS and DIMENSIONS

a   = Horizontal cross-sectional area of packing (ft^2)

A   = Area of air-water interface (ft^2)

C   = Constant

E   = Rate of total heat transfer at a particular point in the packing $\left(\dfrac{Btu}{h}\right)$

E_t = Rate of total heat transfer in the whole of the packing $\left(\dfrac{Btu}{h}\right)$

f   = Driving force correction factor

G   = Air mass flow rate $\left(\dfrac{lb}{h}\right)$

H_g = Enthalpy of bulk air $\left(\dfrac{Btu}{lb\ dry\ air}\right)$

H_{g_1} = Hg at the tower air outlet $\left(\dfrac{Btu}{lb\ dry\ air}\right)$

H_{gm} = Hg at the tower mean position $\left(\dfrac{Btu}{lb\ dry\ air}\right)$

H_{g_2} = Hg at the tower air inlet $\left(\dfrac{Btu}{lb\ dry\ air}\right)$

H_w = Enthalpy of air saturated at the bulk water temperature (°F)

H_{w_1} = H_w at the tower water inlet $\left(\dfrac{Btu}{lb\ dry\ air}\right)$

H_{w_2} = H_w at the tower water outlet $\left(\dfrac{Btu}{lb\ dry\ air}\right)$

H_{wm} = H_w at the "Tower Mean Position" $\left(\dfrac{Btu}{lb\ dry\ air}\right)$

$\triangle H_m$ = Merkel mean driving force $\left(\dfrac{Btu}{lb\ dry\ air}\right)$

K   = Merkel heat transfer coefficient $\left[\dfrac{Btu}{h.ft^2\ (Btu/lb\ dry\ air)}\right]$

K_g = Diffusion coefficient $\left(\dfrac{lb}{h.ft^2\ atm}\right)$

$K^1{}_g$ = Modified diffusion coefficient $\left[\dfrac{lb}{h.ft^2\ (lb\ water/lb\ dry\ air)}\right]$

K_{gs} = Merkel volumetric heat transfer coefficient $\left[\dfrac{Btu}{h.ft^3\ (Btu/lb\ dry\ air)}\right]$

l   = Height of packing (ft)

L   — Water mass flow rate $\left(\dfrac{lb}{h}\right)$

m   = Constant

n   = Constant

P_g = Partial pressure of water vapour in bulk of air (atm.abs)

P_i = Partial pressure of water vapour at air-water interface (atm.abs)

q = Rate of sensible heat transfer $\left(\dfrac{Btu}{h}\right)$

Q = Rate of total heat transfer from water to air $\left(\dfrac{Btu}{h}\right)$

S = Area of contact between the air and water (ft^2)

t = Dry bulb temperature of bulk air (°F)

t_d = Temperature range through which the water is cooled (°F)

t_g = Wet bulb temperature of bulk air (°F)

t_i = Temperature at the air-water interface (°F)

t_w = Temperature of the bulk water (°F)

t_{wm} = Temperature of the bulk water at the "Tower Mean Position" (°F)

t_{wi} = Temperature of the bulk water at the tower inlet (°F)

t_{w2} = Temperature of the bulk water at the tower outlet (°F)

T = Temperature of the bulk water (°F)

W = Water evaporation rate $\left(\dfrac{lb}{h}\right)$

X_g = Absolute humidity of bulk air $\left(\dfrac{lb\ water}{lb\ dry\ air}\right)$

X_i = Absolute humidity of air at the air-water interface $\left(\dfrac{lb\ water}{lb\ dry\ air}\right)$

X_w = Absolute humidity of air saturated at the bulk water temperature $\left(\dfrac{lb\ water}{lb\ dry\ air}\right)$

Y_1 = $H_{w1}-H_{g1}$

Y_2 = $H_{w2}-H_{g2}$

Y_m = $H_{wm}-H_{gm}$

α = Air sensible heat transfer coefficient $\left(\dfrac{Btu}{ft^2\ F°h}\right)$

λ_w = Latent heat of vapourization of water $\left(\dfrac{Btu}{lb}\right)$

CONVERSION TABLE I
Units of Power to British Thermal Units per Hour

ONE HORSE-POWER	2,545 Btu/h
ONE KILOWATT	3,412 Btu/h
ONE KILO-CALORIE/HOUR	3·968 Btu/h
ONE FOOT-POUND/SECOND	4·627 Btu/h
ONE KILOGRAMMETRE/SECOND	33·47 Btu/h

CONVERSION TABLE II
Units of Volume to Imperial Gallons

ONE CUBIC METRE	219·97 gallons
ONE LITRE	0·220 gallons
ONE U.S. GALLON	0·833 gallons
ONE CUBIC FOOT	6·23 gallons

CONVERSION TABLE III
Units of Weight to Pounds Avoirdupois

ONE GRAM	0·0022 lb
ONE KILOGRAM	2·205 lb
ONE TONNE	2,205 lb

CONVERSION TABLE IV

Units of Pressure to Pounds per Square Inch

ONE POUND PER SQUARE FOOT	0·00694 psi
ONE STANDARD ATMOSPHERE	14·696 psi
ONE FOOT HEAD OF WATER 62°F	0·4325 psi
ONE INCH HEAD OF MERCURY 32°F.	0·4912 psi
ONE KILOGRAM/SQ. CENTIMETRE	14·22 psi

CONVERSION TABLE V
Degrees Celsius to Degrees Fahrenheit

C	0°	1°	2°	3°	4°	5°	6°	7°	8°	9°
	°F	°F	°F	°F	°F	°F	°F	°F	°F	°F
0°	32·0	33·8	35·6	37·4	39·2	41·0	42·8	44·6	46·4	48·2
10°	50·0	51·8	53·6	55·4	57·2	59·0	60·8	62·6	64·4	66·2
20°	68·0	69·8	71·6	73·4	75·2	77·0	78·8	80·6	82·4	84·2
30°	86·0	87·8	89·6	91·4	93·2	95·0	96·8	98·6	100·4	102·2
40°	104·0	105·8	107·6	109·4	111·2	113·0	114·8	116·6	118·4	120·2
50°	122·0	123·8	125·6	127·4	129·2	131·0	132·8	134·6	136·4	138·2
60°	140·0	141·8	143·6	145·4	147·2	149·0	150·8	152·6	154·4	156·2
70°	158·0	159·8	161·6	163·4	165·2	167·0	168·8	170·6	172·4	174·2
80°	176·0	177·8	179·6	181·4	183·2	185·0	186·8	188·6	190·4	192·2
90°	194·0	195·8	197·6	199·4	201·2	203·0	204·8	206·6	208·4	210·2
100°	212·0	—	—	—	—	—	—	—	—	—

CONVERSION TABLE VI
Degrees Fahrenheit to Degrees Celsius

F	0°	1°	2°	3°	4°	5°	6°	7°	8°	9°
	°C	°C	°C	°C	°C	°C	°C	°C	°C	°C
30°	—	—	0	0·6	1·1	1·7	2·2	2·8	3·3	3·9
40°	4·4	5·0	5·6	6·1	6·7	7·2	7·8	8·3	8·9	9·4
50°	10·0	10·6	11·1	11·7	12·2	12·8	13·3	13·9	14·4	15·0
60°	15·6	16·1	16·7	17·2	17·8	18·3	18·9	19·4	20·0	20·6
70°	21·1	21·7	22·2	22·8	23·3	23·9	24·4	25·0	25·6	26·1
80°	26·7	27·2	27·8	28·3	28·9	29·4	30·0	30·6	31·1	31·7
90°	32·2	32·8	33·3	33·9	34·4	35·0	35·6	36·1	36·7	37·2
100°	37·8	38·3	38·9	39·4	40·0	40·6	41·1	41·7	42·2	42·8
110°	43·3	43·9	44·4	45·0	45·6	46·1	46·7	47·2	47·8	48·3
120°	48·9	49·4	50·0	50·6	51·1	51·7	52·2	52·8	53·3	53·9
130°	54·4	55·0	55·6	56·1	56·7	57·2	57·8	58·3	58·9	59·4
140°	60·0	60·6	61·1	61·7	62·2	62·8	63·3	63·9	64·4	65·0
150°	65·6	66·1	66·7	67·2	67·8	68·3	68·9	69·4	70·0	70·6
160°	71·1	71·7	72·2	72·8	73·3	73·9	74·4	75·0	75·6	76·1
170°	76·7	77·2	77·8	78·3	78·9	79·4	80·0	80·6	81·1	81·7
180°	82·2	82·8	83·3	83·9	84·4	85·0	85·6	86·1	86·7	87·2
190°	87·8	88·3	88·9	89·4	90·0	90·6	91·1	91·7	92·2	92·8
200°	93·3	93·9	94·4	95·0	95·6	96·1	96·7	97·2	97·8	98·3
210°	98·9	99·4	100·0	—	—	—	—	—	—	—

TABLE VII

HARDNESS OF WATER   :   CONVERSION OF UNITS

Clark's Scale: Degrees	Parts per Million	Parts per Million	Clark's Scale: Degrees
0	0	0	0
1	14	10	0·7
2	29	20	1·4
3	43	30	2·1
4	57	40	2·8
5	71	50	3·5
6	86	60	4·2
7	100	70	4·9
8	114	80	5·6
9	129	90	6·3
10	143	100	7·0
11	157	110	7·7
12	171	120	8·4
13	186	130	9·1
14	200	140	9·8
15	214	150	10·5
16	229	160	11·2
17	243	170	11·9
18	257	180	12·6
19	271	190	13·3
20	286	200	14·0
30	429	300	21·0
40	571	400	28·0
50	714	500	35·0

The generally accepted classification of waters is as follows:—

	Parts per Million	Parts per 100,000	Degrees Clark
Soft	0 to 50	0 to 5	0 to 3·5
Moderately soft	50 to 100	5 to 10	3·5 to 7·0
Slightly hard	100 to 150	10 to 15	7·0 to 10·5
Moderately hard...	150 to 200	15 to 20	10·5 to 14·0
Hard	200 to 300	20 to 30	14·0 to 21·0
Very hard	Over 300	Over 30	Over 21·0

The hardness, permanent and temporary, is expressed in terms of calcium carbonate; that is, it is the calcium carbonate equivalent of the content of calcium and magnesium salts in the water.

$$1 \text{ degree on Clark's scale} = 1 \text{ grain per gallon.}$$
$$= 1 \text{ part per } 70,000.$$
$$= 1\cdot43 \text{ parts per } 100,000.$$
$$= 14\cdot3 \text{ parts per million.}$$

TABLE 12

Background sound pressure levels

ENVIRONMENT	Sound pressure level (dBA)
EMPTY CHURCH	30
UNOCCUPIED PRIVATE RESIDENCE ..	35
LIBRARY	40
QUIET PRIVATE OFFICE	45
QUIET RESTAURANT	50
QUIET SHOP	55
GENERAL OFFICE	60
AVERAGE OCCUPIED RESTAURANT ..	65
MECHANISED OFFICE	70
NOISY RESTAURANT	75
FACTORY MACHINE SHOP	80
UNDERGROUND TRAIN	85
NOISY FACTORY	90
AIRCRAFT CABIN	95
SHIP'S SIREN AT 100 ft...	100
BOILER PLATE CONSTRUCTION SHOP ..	110

TABLE 13

Water flow capacities in gallons per hour for various sizes of pipe and speeds of flow

Pipe bore in inches	WATER SPEED IN FEET PER SECOND						
	2	4	6	8	10	12	14
	GALLONS PER HOUR						
$\frac{1}{4}$	15	30	46	61	76	92	105
$\frac{3}{8}$	34	69	103	137	172	206	238
$\frac{1}{2}$	61	122	184	245	306	368	427
$\frac{5}{8}$	94	190	285	380	474	570	658
$\frac{3}{4}$	138	276	414	552	690	828	966
1	245	490	735	980	1225	1470	1715
$1\frac{1}{4}$	382	765	1150	1530	1910	2300	2674
$1\frac{1}{2}$	550	1100	1650	2200	2750	3300	3850
2	980	1960	2940	3920	4900	5880	6860
$2\frac{1}{2}$	1530	3060	4590	6120	7650	9180	10710
3	2200	4410	6620	8820	11000	13240	15400
4	3920	7840	11750	15700	19600	23500	27440
5	6120	12250	18350	24500	30600	36700	42840
6	8800	17600	26400	35200	44000	52800	61600
7	12000	24000	36000	48000	60000	72000	84000
8	15680	31360	47040	62720	78400	94080	109760

INDEX